You Can't Love God With A Dirty Bathroom!

How to Reveal your Love to God, Yourself and Others

MICHAEL R. WHITE

Scripture quotations are
from the King James Version of the Bible.

Spreading The Word Publishing
P.O. Box 2253
Upper Marlboro, MD 20773-2253
301-574-2507

Book Cover Illustration, David Middleton, DM Designs

Copyright © by 2001 by Michael R. White

All rights reserved. This book, or parts thereof, may not be reproduced in any form without permission.

Library of Congress Cataloging-in-Publication Data
Michael R. White

Library of Congress Control Number: 2001126659
ISBN 0-9714069-0-1

Printed in the United States of America

Dedication

I dedicate this book to my wife, help meet, lover and best friend, Gina Marie White.

Acknowledgements

First and foremost I want to thank God the Father for *creating* me, God the Son (Jesus Christ) for *dying* for me and God the Holy Spirit for guiding me.

Throughout the process of writing this book, God has placed people in my life to assist me in spreading the gospel of Jesus Christ. The following is a list of "heaven sent" people for which I will be eternally grateful:

- ✞ Gina, Brandyn and Brian for supporting me every step of the way.

- ✞ Chip Tyler and Syrita Blount for providing me with the foundational teachings of the Spread the Word newsletters.

- ✞ Deborah Harrison, Heather Mackall and Wendy Tonic for providing copy editing services.

- ✞ Petra Martin for providing marketing research.

- ✞ Christopher "Melchizedek" Robinson for assisting me in bringing this book to market.

- ✞ Gloria Gilbert, GG Designs for providing desktop publishing and copy editing services.

- ✞ David Middleton, DM Designs, Peter Newman, Choice Publications and Janice Chika, Copy Connections for designing the book cover.

- ✞ Family and friends of the Spread the Word Ministry for their spiritual and financial support.

Contents

	Introduction vii
Chapter One:	Love 1
Chapter Two:	How Do We Love and Why? 7
Chapter Three:	How Do We Love God Through Obedience? 13
Chapter Four:	How Do We Love God Through Sacrifice? 19
Chapter Five:	How Do We Love God Through Stewardship? 25
Chapter Six:	How Do We Love Ourselves? 31
Chapter Seven:	How Do We Love Our Parents? 39
Chapter Eight:	How Do We Love Our Spouse? 45
Chapter Nine:	How Do We Love Our Children? 59
Chapter Ten:	How Do We Love Our Employer? 67
Chapter Eleven:	How Do We Love Our Friends? 73
Chapter Twelve:	How Do We Love Our Enemies? 83
	Encouragement and Advice 91
	Biblical References by Chapter 95
	About the Author 101

Introduction

I know what you are thinking, what does a dirty bathroom have to do with loving God? I thought the same thing when God woke me up at 4 o'clock in the morning to clean my master bathroom, which by the way, needed a good scrubbing.

While I was on my hands and knees cleaning the shower, I heard the voice of God say, **"You can't love Me with a dirty bathroom."** At first I ignored Him. I thought my mind was playing tricks on me or the fumes from the cleaning solution were causing me to hallucinate. As I finished my early morning chore, God spoke again, **"You can't love Me with a dirty bathroom."** This time I paid close attention to what He was saying.

God reminded me of the series of exhortation newsletters I wrote dealing with the topic of "Love", specifically the September 1999 issue entitled, *"How to Love God through Stewardship."* In this newsletter, I wrote that God is the Creator and Owner of all that exists, which is taken from John 1:13 and Psalms 24:1, respectively. Since we as human beings did not create or own anything, that would make us managers or stewards.

Webster's Dictionary defines steward(ship) as "an individual's responsibility to manage his life and property with proper regard to the rights of others." Simply put, we are merely managers, not owners, over that which God has placed in our possession.

What God was reminding me was that **one** of the ways to reveal our love towards Him is by properly maintaining and managing those people, places and things (houses, cars, furniture, jobs and children, etc.) with which He has blessed us. When we service our car(s) on a timely basis, arrive to work on time, hang up our clothes, dust the furniture and yes, clean our bathrooms, we let God know through our actions and not just our words, how much we truly love and appreciate all that He has done, is doing and will do for us.

Although the title of this book specifically addresses the principle of stewardship (*chapter 5*), **"You Can't Love God with a Dirty Bathroom"** will teach us the many different ways to love God, others and ourselves.

"You Can't Love God with a Dirty Bathroom" is a compilation of monthly newsletters from my exhortation ministry, Spread The Word, which I began in July 1996. Between January 1999 and December 2000, God instructed me to write about one topic, "Love." The two-year's worth of writings constitutes this one book.

The purpose of **"You Can't Love God with a Dirty Bathroom,"** as well as the Spread The Word Ministry is to:

➤ Enable the unsaved to have the seed of God's Word planted in their heart and mind.

➤ Give new converts the desire to learn God's Word.

➤ Encourage seasoned Christians to increase their knowledge of God's Word.

The ultimate goal of this book is to:

➤ Give you a greater understanding of God's Word.

➤ Draw you closer to God and His Word.

➤ Encourage you to study, live by, and share God's Word.

Since all of the information contained in this book is based on God's Word, you, the reader, must accept the Bible as the inherent Word of God, written by holy men and women of God, inspired by the Holy Spirit. **"You Can't Love God with a Dirty Bathroom"** and the Spread the Word newsletters are not substitutes for the Bible, but are merely and humbly a "clear path" to the Word of God.

At the end of each chapter, I have included several exercises designed to strengthen your knowledge and comprehension of the text. There is also an opportunity to exegesis or fully interpret a selected scripture, applicable to the chapter topic. Exegesis is the critical interpretation of Bible text. It is by which we can correctly interpret the Word of God.

The following is a list of the steps to **exegesis** or **interpret** the highlighted scripture:

1. Pray. God's Word is divine and as humans we are limited. We must pray to God to receive a fresh illumination of His Word.

2. Read the verse of scripture and write down your interpretation of its meaning.

3. Determine the literary style of the verse, if applicable.

4. Define the key words in the verse by using your biblical references (e.g. concordance).

5. Based upon the new information you gathered, write down a second interpretation of the verse.

6. Once you receive a complete understanding of the verse, apply it to a specific situation in your life, whether it's a past, present or future experience. By doing this, you'll have a frame of reference to remind you of how God's Word assisted you in your Christian walk.

7. Finally, thank God for the opportunity to have received a greater understanding of His Word.

You Can't Love God With A Dirty Bathroom!

Because it's a direct interpretation of the Hebrew and Greek writings, I strongly encourage you to use a King James Version of the Bible. I also recommend that you use the *New Strong's Exhaustive Concordance of the Bible* along with Webster's Dictionary to complete these exercises

Chapter 1

Love

Beloved, let us love one another: for love is of God; and every one that loveth is born of God, and knoweth God. He that loveth not knoweth not God; for God is love.

1 John 4: 7–8

Whether in past or present tense, the word *love* is used over 400 times throughout the Bible and has several meanings and translations. Within the New Testament, the majority of these meanings stem from two Greek words; "agape" and "phileo".

Agape describes God's attitude toward His Son and those who accept Jesus as their personal Lord and Savior. It also conveys God's will to His children concerning their feelings toward one another and toward all men. Agape expresses the essential nature of God.

Phileo differs from agape in that it focuses on our relationship with humankind. Phileo conveys a feeling of fondness and tender affection for someone (not necessarily in a sexual sense).

The following scriptures provide a clear distinction between the meanings of agape and phileo:

*"For God so **loved** the world, that he gave his only begotten Son, that whosoever believeth in him should not perish, but have everlasting life." - John 3:16*

*"Be kindly affectioned one to another with brotherly **love**; in honour preferring one another." - Romans 12:10*

John 3:16 illustrates God's unconditional love for mankind, whereas in Romans 12:10, Apostle Paul gives the believer instructions on how to love *each other.*

What is Love?

Simply put, God is Love. John the Apostle teaches us if we do not love one another, we can't know God, because He is love. 1 John 4:8 reads:

"He that loveth not knoweth not God; for God is love."

God and love are one. They are inherent to one another, meaning they are essential, necessary and critical to each other's existence. One could not exist without the other; similar to water and wet. Water could not be water without its being wet.

The following is a list of words that best describe love and how we should exercise our feelings of love:

➢ **Unconditional Love** — *"For God so **loved** the world, that he gave his only begotten Son, that whosoever believeth in Him should not perish, but have everlasting life." -* John 3:16. God gave us His greatest gift, asking for nothing in return. How many times do we give or do something for someone expecting some type of recognition? Is this true love?

> **Sacrificial Love** — In John 3:16, God's love for us was so strong that He sacrificed His only Son, so that anyone who believed in Him would not die a spiritual death. What or who are we willing to give up to demonstrate our love for God?

> **Obedient Love** — *"He that hath my commandments, and keepeth them, he it is that loveth me: and he that loveth me shall be loved of my Father, and I will love him, and will manifest myself to him."* - John 14:21. If we truly love God, will we obey and follow His instructions, laws and commandments?

> **Forgiving Love** — *"If we confess our sins, he is faithful and just to forgive us our sins, and to cleanse us from all unrighteousness." - 1 John 1:9.* God loves us so much that He will forgive us of our sins, if we acknowledge and truly repent or "to turn from" of our sins.

In Matthew 6:14-15, Jesus teaches us that we must forgive others before we can be forgiven of our sins. It is easy to ask God for forgiveness, but difficult to grant it to others. Whenever we ask God to forgive us for a sin that we have committed, we should ask ourselves, have I forgiven the people who have hurt me?

In Hebrew 10:17, God's word also reads that He will not remember our "sins and iniquities." We cannot truly forgive someone if we constantly remind ourselves and/or them of their wrongdoing.

> **Patient Love** — *"Now we exhort you, brethren, warn them that are unruly, comfort the feebleminded, support the weak, be patient toward all men..." - 1 Thessalonians 5:14.* Paul teaches us to forbear or have patience with one another's faults and weaknesses. How many times has God withheld his wrath from us and exercised patience

over our shortcomings, especially when we deserved to be punished?

➤ **Tough (Correcting) Love** — *"For whom the Lord loveth he correcteth; even as a father the son in whom he delighteth."* - Proverbs 3:12. God loves us so much that He is willing to correct our behavior before we suffer the consequences of our actions. How many of us are willing to lose a friend in order to save them?

➤ **Never-Ending Love** — *"O give thanks unto the Lord; for he is good: for his mercy endureth forever."* - Psalms 136:1. Repeated throughout this entire Psalm is the phrase, *"for his mercy endureth forever,"* which reminds us that God's love for us is everlasting and like Him, unchanging. Can we say this about our love for God, our family and/or friends?

It's important to note that a feeling of love must be followed by an action. For example, ***"For God so loved the world"*** is the attitude (feeling) God has toward us. ***"He gave His only begotten Son"*** is the outward manifestation (action) of His love for us. We could not have been saved from sin just by God telling us He loved us. An expression or action of His love for us had to follow His feeling of love. Just like faith, love without works is dead!

Biblical References

1 Corinthians 13:4
Galatians 6:10
2 John 1:6
Hebrews 12:6

Romans 5:8
1 John 4:7
Matthew 6:14-15

Assignment
LOVE

1. What are the three ways God expresses His love toward us?

2. Based on God's definition of love, are we able to truly forgive, but not forget what a person did to hurt us? (Explain)

3. What is the difference between agape and phileo?

4. Now that we have a better understanding of the meaning of "unconditional love", let's apply what we have learned. Chose someone for whom you are going to do a good deed. Pray and ask God to reveal to you something that person needs. In order to demonstrate your unconditional love for this person, you must perform the deed anonymously.

By using the steps outlined in the introduction of this book, interpret the bold words in the following scripture, Romans 8:35–39:

"Who shall **separate** us from the **love** of Christ? shall **tribulation** or **distress**, or **persecution**, or **famine**, or **nakedness**, or **peril**, or **sword**? As it is written, For thy sake we are killed all the day long; we are accounted as sheep for the slaughter. **Nay**, in all these things we are more than **conquerors** through him that loved us. For I am persuaded, that neither **death**, nor **life**, nor **angels**, nor **principalities**, nor **powers**, nor things present, nor things to come, Nor **height**, nor **depth**, nor any other **creature**, shall be able to separate us from the love of God, which is in Christ Jesus our Lord."

Chapter 2

How Do We Love And Why?

"For when we were yet without strength, in due time Christ died for the ungodly. For scarcely for a righteous man will one die: yet peradventure for a good man some would even dare to die. But God commendeth his love toward us, in that, while we were yet sinners, Christ died for us."

Romans 5:6-8

In chapter one, we learned the true meaning of the word "love." We learned that God is love and those who do not love one another can not know God, because He is love (1 John 4:8). In this chapter, we will learn how to love and why we should love.

In the book of John, Jesus teaches us that we are to love one another as He loved us. John 15:12 reads:

*"This is my commandment, That ye love **one another**, as I have loved you."*

This commandment can be difficult to follow if we do not know how Jesus loves us.

How does Jesus love us?

Jesus loved us so much that He humbled Himself and left His throne in heaven to walk among us and become a living, breathing example of righteousness. Philippians 2:5-8 reads:

> *"Let this mind be in you, which was also in Christ Jesus. Who, being in the form of God, thought it not robbery to be equal with God: But made himself of no reputation, and took upon him the form of a servant, and was made in the likeness of men: And being found in fashion as a man, he **humbled** himself..."*

Jesus removed His royal crown and came "down" to meet us at our level. In order for us to be sons and daughters of God, we must *"have the same mind as Christ"* and leave our comfort zone to lend a helping hand to those in need.

Secondly, Jesus demonstrated His love for us by living a life according to His own Word. He set an example on how to live a righteous life. 1 Peter 2:21-23 reads:

> *"For even hereunto were ye called: because Christ also suffered for us, leaving us an **example**, that ye should follow his steps: Who did no sin, neither was guile [deceit] found in his mouth: Who, when he was reviled [called bad named], reviled not again; when he suffered, he threatened not; but committed himself to him that judgeth righteously..."*

Jesus Christ **chose** to live a life of righteousness, without sin, despite being verbally insulted and physically abused. Once we become a new creature in Christ, we have the same opportunity to lead others to the Body of Christ by being an example for them to follow.

In addition to Jesus being a righteous example, He "laid down" His life for us. Jesus bore our sins and was offered up as the ultimate sacrifice to save us from a life of damnation. 1 John 3:16 reads:

"Hereby perceive we the love of God, because he laid down his life for us: and we ought to lay down our lives for the brethren."

Jesus teaches us that there is no greater love that we can show than by putting the lives of others before our own selfish wants and desires. Jesus says in John 15:13:

"Greater love hath no man than this, that a man lay down his life for his friends."

We can lay down our lives by helping when it is not convenient, by giving when it hurts, or by devoting energy to others' problems or circumstances instead of merely our own. (Philippians 2:3-4)

Lastly, Jesus loved us so much that He promised us that He would not leave us alone. The Holy Spirit was sent to continue Jesus' earthly ministry, as we read in John 14:15-16,18:

*"If ye love me, keep my commandments. And I will pray the Father, and he shall give you another **Comforter** (Holy Spirit), that he may abide with you for ever; I will not leave you comfortless: I will come to you."*

In the context of the scripture, the Greek translation of *comforter* is "parakletos", which means "intercessor." Following to Jesus' death, God the Father sent the Holy Spirit to intercede on our behalf and to continue to teach us how to live a righteous life. Unlike Jesus in His human form, the Holy Spirit will live in us, as well as dwell among us.

Why Should We Love?

We should love because, just like God, we are love! When God first created the human spirit, He made us in the likeness and image of Himself (Genesis 1:26). Therefore, if God is love and we are made in His image, we are "love," as well.

In order to tap into that love, we must accept Jesus Christ as our personal Lord and Savior and allow the Spirit of God to dwell in us. Once God's Spirit lives in us, He will cause us to obey His commandments. Ezekiel 36:27 reads:

*"And I will put my **spirit** in you, and **cause** you to walk in my statutes, and ye shall keep my judgments, and do them."*

By obeying the commandments of God and demonstrating our love for others, the world will know that we are Christians. The words that Jesus spoke to His disciples in John 13:34-35 applies to us today:

*"A new commandment I give unto you, That ye love one another; as I loved you, that ye also love one another. By this **shall all men know** that ye are my disciples, if ye have love one to another."*

Jesus teaches that our Christ-like love for one another will reveal that we are His disciples.

Do people see us plagued with envy, bitterness, jealously and strife in our home, church or workplace? Or do they know we are Christians because of our attitude toward others? Allow the manifestation of Jesus Christ to show in our lives, by loving one another.

Biblical References

1 John 3:11
John 1:14
1 John 3:18
2 Corinthians 5:21

1 John 3:15
Romans 5:8
John 13:35

Assignment
How Do I Love and Why?

1. When Jesus was verbally insulted and physically attacked, how did He respond? (1 Peter 2:21-23)

2. Prior to His crucifixion, Jesus promised His disciples He would not leave them alone. Jesus said He would pray to the Father and ask Him to send "another Comforter." Who is this other Comforter? How long will He be with us? (John 14:16)

3. How does Jesus want us to love others? (John 13:34-35)

4. In John 15:13, Jesus teaches us that no greater love can be demonstrated than to lay down our lives for our friends. We may not have to die for someone, as Jesus did, but we can sacrifice or weaken our fleshly desires, while strengthening someone else's spirit.

Pray to God and ask Him to reveal unto you an area in your life that may be causing a family member, friend, co-worker or complete stranger to turn away from God. Once you have identified this area or areas, make a commitment unto the Lord that **no longer will the words you speak, the things you do, the places you go or the people with whom**

you associate, cause another to stumble and turn away from God.

By using the steps outlined in the introduction of this book, interpret the bold words in the following scripture, 1 Corinthians 13:4:

"**Charity suffereth long**, and is **kind**; charity **envieth** not; charity **vaunteth** not itself, is not **puffed** up..."

Chapter 3

How Do We Love God Through Obedience?

"He that hath my commandments, and keepeth them, he it is that loveth me: and he that loveth me shall be loved of my Father, and I will love him, and will manifest myself to him."

John 14:21

The love we show towards God, as well as others, must be revealed through our actions and not by our words alone. 1 John 3:18 reads:

> *"My little children, let us not love in word, neither in tongue; but in deed and in truth."*

God is not interested in lip service. Remember, it was God who confirmed His love for us by *offering* His only begotten son to be a sacrifice for our sins.

Jesus teaches us that we reveal our love for God by receiving and obeying His Word. John 14:21a reads:

> *"He that hath my commandments, and keepeth them, he it is that loveth me..."*

We express our love for Jesus by obeying His commandments and instructions. As I stated earlier, love is more than kind words. It is a commitment to those words and the action that follows. If we love Christ, we must prove it by obeying His Word.

Many people diligently study and comprehend God's Word, but fail to apply it to their everyday lives. We deceive ourselves if we say we love God and *choose* not to obey His Word.

In many situations, we will be called upon to obey God's commandments without full understanding. Not only does this test our faith in God, it will challenge the degree to which we love God.

In the 22nd chapter of Genesis, God tests Abraham's willingness to obey His instructions. The first verse reads:

"And it came to pass after these things, that God did tempt [test] Abraham, and said unto him, Abraham: and he said, Behold, here I am."

God instructed Abraham to offer his son Isaac for a burnt offering. Without hesitation, Abraham prepared a place to make this unusual offering to God.

Genesis 22:2–3 reads:

"And he said, Take now thy son, thine only son Isaac, whom thou lovest, and get thee into the land of Moriah; and offer him there for a burnt offering upon one of the mountains which I will tell thee of."

"And Abraham rose early in the morning, and saddled his ass, and took two of his young men with him, and Isaac his son, and clave [split] the wood for the burnt offering, and rose up, and went unto the place of which God had told him."

As Abraham was about to slay his son, an angel appeared and stopped him from completing the sacrifice. We read in Genesis 22:10-12:

*"And Abraham stretched forth his hand, and took the knife to slay his son. And the angel of the Lord called unto him out of heaven, and said, Abraham, Abraham: and he said, Here am I. And he said, Lay not thine hand upon the lad, neither do thou any thing unto him: for now I know that thou **fearest** God, seeing thou hast not withheld thy son, thine only son from me."*

In the context of this scripture the Hebrew translation of *fearest* is "yare," which means reverent, worshipful or adoring. As a result of Abraham's fear or adoration for God and his willingness to demonstrate his love, Isaac was spared and an animal was sacrificed in his place. Genesis 22:13 tells us:

"And Abraham lifted up his eyes, and looked, and behold behind him a ram caught in a thicket by his horns: and Abraham went and took the ram, and offered him up for a burnt offering in the stead of his son."

God had no desire to harm Isaac. The purpose of this test was to strengthen Abraham's character and love for God. As a result of his experience, Abraham deepened his dedication to obey God.

Until we are faced with challenges such as Abraham's, we will never know the degree to which we love God and we will continue to find it difficult to love God beyond our words.

The Benefits of Loving God through Obedience

Throughout the Bible we learn of God's omnipotent, omnipresent and omniscient power. As we obey God's commandments God will protect us from danger seen and unseen. He will safely guide us into the future and teach us all things.

Because of Abraham's obedience, God promised to multiply his descendants upon the face of the earth. God also promised to protect them from their enemies and called them blessed throughout the land. According to Genesis 22:15-19:

> *"And the angel of the Lord called unto Abraham out of heaven the second time, And said, By myself have I sworn, saith the Lord, for because thou hast done this thing, and hast not withheld thy son, thine only son: That in blessing I will bless thee, and in multiplying I will multiply thy seed as the stars of the heaven, and as the sand which is upon the seashore; and thy seed shall possess the gate of his enemies; And in thy seed shall all the nations of the earth be blessed; because thou hast obeyed my voice."*

God eagerly awaits to bestow his blessings upon us. We must decide in our heart if we love and trust God enough to receive His blessings.

Biblical References

Romans 12:9　　　　　1 John 2:4
Proverbs 2:6-7　　　　James 1:2-3
2 Corinthians 5:7　　　James 2:20
Proverbs 3:1-2

Assignment
How To Love God through Obedience?

1. In John 14:21, Jesus teaches us that if we **love** Him, we will keep His commandments. What is the definition of love? (1 John 4:8)

2. In the early chapters of Genesis, Moses shares the story of Adam and Eve and God's original plan for their lives. How did Adam and Eve disobey God's Word? Who did Adam and Eve blame for their disobedience? Who should be held accountable for their actions? (Genesis chapter 2–3)

3. In Genesis 22:1, God tested Abraham's love and commitment to Him. How did God test Abraham's faith in Him? Did Abraham pass the test?

4. In this chapter, we learned that in some situations we may have to obey God without full understanding. In order to demonstrate his love for God, Abraham was instructed to sacrifice his son, Isaac.

What instructions and/or commandments has God given you that you did not fully understand? Ask the Holy Spirit to bring to your remembrance that situation. Write down as much of the experience as you can remember, then answer the following questions: What was my attitude and/or feeling towards God's instructions? Did I immediately obey or did I hesitate to respond? If I obeyed, what reward(s) did I receive? If I did not, what consequences did I experience?

Allow each situation to prepare your heart for the next time you are tested by God.

By using the steps outlined in the introduction of this book, interpret the bold words in the following scripture, Proverbs 2:1–2,5:

"My son, if thou wilt **receive** my **words**, and **hide** my **commandments** with thee; So that thou **incline** thine **ear** unto **wisdom**, and **apply** thine **heart** to **understanding**: Then shalt thou understand the **fear** of the Lord, and **find** the **knowledge** of God."

Chapter 4

How Do We Love God through Sacrifice?

"For he hath made him to be sin for us, who knew no sin; that we might be made the righteousness of God in him."

2 Corinthians 5:21

In the previous chapter, we learned how to love God through our obedience to His word. Jesus teaches us that we reveal our love for Him by receiving and obeying His commandments (John 14:21a).

The story of Abraham preparing his son Isaac as a sacrifice for God is an extraordinary example of obeying God's instructions, despite not having full understanding of the situation.

As a result of Abraham's obedience, God promised to multiply his descendants upon the face of the earth and protect them from their enemies (Genesis 22:1-24).

In this chapter we will learn how to love God through sacrifice and what the benefits are to making such a sacrifice.

The Example We Must Follow

The most powerful and profound verse of scripture in the Bible tells of God's extraordinary demonstration of His love for us. John 3:16 reads:

> *"For God so loved the world, that He **gave** His only begotten Son, that whosover believeth in Him should not perish, but have everlasting life."*

In the context of this scripture, the Greek translation of *gave* is "didomi", which means to yield or sacrifice. In order to demonstrate His love for us, God gave up a part of Himself, instructed His Son, Jesus to lay on the cross and die for our sins.

The shedding of Jesus' blood represents our redemption from sin. Hebrews 9:11-14 reads:

> *"But Christ being come an high priest of good things to come, by a greater and more perfect tabernacle, not made with hands, that is to say, not of this building; Neither by the blood of goats and calves, but by his own blood he entered in once into the holy place, having obtained eternal redemption for us. For if the blood of bulls and of goats, and the ashes of an heifer sprinkling the unclean, sanctifieth to the purifying of the flesh: How much more shall the blood of Christ, who through the eternal Spirit offered Himself without spot of God, purge your conscience from dead works to serve the living God?"*

Jesus Christ ransomed and sacrificed His life, so that all who believe in Him will not die, but will have everlasting life.

God sets the pattern of true love, the foundation for all relationships. If we truly love someone, we must be willing to give freely to the point of self-sacrifice. **GOD SURE DID!**

How Do I Love God through Sacrifice?

We reveal our love for God by sacrificing or giving ourselves to God, as God gave himself to us.

Apostle Paul instructs us to offer ourselves as a "living sacrifice," pure and well pleasing unto God. As he wrote in Romans 12:1:

"I beseech you therefore, brethren, by the mercies of God, that ye present your bodies a living sacrifice, holy, acceptable unto God, which is your reasonable service."

In addition, Jesus teaches us that we must sacrifice our own selfish desires and be prepared to suffer for His sake. Mark 8:34b reads:

"Whosoever will come after me, let him deny himself, and take up his cross and follow me."

In the context of this scripture, the Greek translation of deny is "aparneomai," which means to disown or abstain. If we truly and sincerely love God, we must bring our flesh under subjection and allow our spirit to be guided by God and His Word.

Apostle Paul teaches us that when we accept Jesus Christ as our personal Lord and Savior, we become new beings, both internally and externally, thus allowing the old things, people, activities and feelings to pass away. In 2 Corinthians 5:17–18a he writes:

> *"Therefore if any man be in Christ, he is a new creature: old things are passed away; behold, all things are become new. And all things are of God, who hath reconciled us to Himself by Jesus Christ..."*

We can no longer do those things; associate with those people; participate in those activities or express those emotions (pride, lust, envy, etc) that please our flesh and displease God.

Unfortunately, too many "so-called" Christians keep one foot in the world and one foot in the Body of Christ. Some of us are not willing to completely relinquish our old ways and accept our new role in Christ Jesus.

As members of the Body of Christ, we have the opportunity to be washed clean of our past life with the blood of Jesus and have the distinct honor and privilege to give God our most precious gift, ourselves.

What Are the Benefits of Sacrifice?

Jesus teaches us that if we are willing to give up our desires for His sake, as well as the gospel's, He will protect and preserve our life. Mark 8:35 reads,

> *"For whosoever will save his life shall lose it; but whosoever shall lose his life for my sake and the gospel's, the same shall save it."*

In the context of this scripture the Greek translation of save is "sozo," which means to preserve or protect. The translation of lose is "apollumi," which means to destroy. Although this verse of scripture is somewhat confusing to read, Jesus makes it perfectly clear that He wants us to choose to follow Him rather than continue to please our flesh and lead a life of sin. Jesus wants us to stop trying to control our own destiny and let Him lead, guide and direct us. This makes good sense because, as the Creator, He knows better than we do what's best for us.

Biblical References

2 John 6
Romans 6:12a-13
2 Corinthians 5:17
Revelation 1:5

Romans 8:32
Luke 14:27
John 12:25

Assignment
How To Love God through Sacrifice?

1. As it relates to sacrifices, what was the purpose of the shedding of animal blood in the Old Testament and the shedding of Jesus' blood in the New Testament? (Hebrews 9:11-14)

2. According to Jesus, what three things must we do to "come after" Him? (Mark 8:34b)

3. How did God demonstrate His extraordinary love for us? (John 3:16).

4. This exercise will enable us to examine our actions as a member of the Body of Christ. Review 2 Corinthians 5:17-18, where Apostle Paul teaches if any man be in Christ Jesus, he is a new creature, all the old things are passed away.

Take out a blank sheet of paper and draw a line down the middle of the page, creating two columns. At the top of the left column, write **"OLD THINGS."** At the top of the right column write **"NEW CREATURE."** Beneath **"OLD THINGS"**, make a list of all the sins you committed prior to accepting Jesus Christ as your personal Lord and Savior.

This might include such things as lying, cheating, stealing, fornicating, gossiping, etc. (*I encourage you to read Romans 1:18-32, concerning God's anger towards sin.*)

Once you have completed this task, review the list and cross out the sins you have overcome. Next, identify the sins you are still committing and write them in the **"NEW CREATURE"** column. Lastly, complete the following steps:

1. Think about the devastating effects these sins are having on your life and those around you.

2. Acknowledge (confess) your sins to God.

3. Ask for forgiveness and repent of these sins.

By using the steps outlined in the introduction of this book, interpret the bold words in the following scripture, Romans 1:29-31:

> "Being **filled** with all **unrighteousness, fornication, wickedness, covetousness, maliciousness**; full of **envy, murder, debate, deceit, malignity; whisperers, Backbiters, haters** of God, **despiteful, proud, boasters, inventors** of evil things, **disobedient** to parents, Without understanding, **conventbreakers**, without **natural affection, implacable, unmerciful.**"

Chapter 5

How Do We Love God Through Stewardship?

"And the Lord said, Who then is that faithful and wise steward, whom his lord shall make rule over his household, to give them their portion of meat in due season?"

Luke 12:42

In chapters 3 and 4 we learned how to love God through obedience and sacrifice, respectively. In this chapter we will examine how to reveal our love for God, who is the creator and owner of all, through stewardship over the things for which He has blessed us.

God, Creator of All

Simply put, God is the creator of all that we see, touch, smell, hear, and think. John 1:3 reads:

*"All things were **made** by him; and without him was not any thing made that was made."*

In the context of this scripture, the Hebrew translation of *made* or *create*, as it relates to God, means to "bring into existence or being". For instance, when darkness fell upon the earth, God created light (Genesis 1:3). Chapters 1 and 2 of the book of Genesis provides a detailed description of how and in what order God created all things (e.g. light, space, land, water, grass, animals and humans, etc).

When God created, He made something from nothing by speaking it into existence (e.g. light). As created beings, we do not have the power to create anything. When we as humans invent or make something, we use that which God has already created.

God, Owner of All

As the creator of all things, God is also the owner of all things. Psalms 24:1 reads:

> *"The earth is the Lord's, and the **fulness** thereof; the world, and they that dwell therein."*

The Hebrew translation of *fulness* in this context is "melow", which means "all that is". God is the sole owner of everything that He created both seen and unseen.

If God is **THE** creator and owner of all things, what are we?

We are **Stewards!**

Because the earth is the Lord's and all that live above it, upon it and beneath it, we are stewards or managers of God's possessions.

Webster defines stewardship as "an individual's responsibility to **manage** his life and property with proper regard to the rights of others." We are merely managers not owners, of that which God has placed in our possession.

I liken this relationship between God and man to the lease agreement between an owner of an apartment building and the renter. The owner or property manager of that apartment complex establishes the rules and regulations for living in that community. These rules may include; what time of the month rent payments are due, noise ordinances, pet ownership, how many visitor parking spaces will made available to each tenant, etc....

Once the tenant signs the lease agreement, he or she is subject to the rules established by the true owner of the property. In many cases, the tenant must seek approval from the owner/property manager prior to re-painting the walls, hanging a picture or laying down new carpet.

If the tenant does not abide by the rules set forth in the lease agreement, the owner/property manager has the right to terminate the contract and evict the tenant from the apartment, thus relinquishing them of their stewardship over the property.

How Do I Love God through Stewardship?

We reveal our love for God through stewardship by developing and maintaining that which God has given to us.

Subsequent to being placed in the Garden of Eden, Adam was given four instructions by God: 1) work and serve in the garden; 2) maintain the garden; 3) protect the garden; and 4) not to eat any fruit from a certain tree in the garden. As Genesis 2:15-16 tells us:

"And the Lord God took the man, and put him into the garden of Eden to dress (work) it and to keep (maintain) it. And the Lord God commanded the man, saying, of every tree of the garden thou mayest freely eat: But of the tree of the knowledge of good and evil, thou shalt not eat of it: for in the day that thou eatest thereof thou shalt surely die."

The garden created by God was the environment enabling Adam and his family to live, grow and prosper. For us, the "garden" represents our home, place of employment and all other items with which God has blessed us.

Just like Adam, God expects us not only to maintain and protect our environment, but obey the rules He has set forth or face the same consequences as Adam.

How can we say we love God, when He has blessed us with a home that we refuse to clean; a job for which we are consistently late; a car that we continue to run, never replacing its oil; a spouse we abuse; a child we refuse to train; a body that we will fill with smoke, drugs and alcohol; a mind that we refuse to educate and a spirit that is not fed the Word of God?

What are Benefits of Godly Stewardship?

As a result of our proper stewardship or management over God's possessions, we gain the trust of God as well as receive additional responsibilities. In Matthew 25:14-30, Jesus tells the parable of the **loaned money**.

Prior to traveling, a master gave different amounts of money to each of his three servants. One servant was given five talents, one received two talents and the last servant was given one talent. The master divided the money (talents) among his servants according to their abilities (v.15). In other words, no one received more or less than he could handle.

Once the master continued on his journey, the servants that received five and two talents doubled their money by putting the money to work (like The Stock Market). The servant that received one talent buried his money in the ground (v.16-18).

When the master returned, he settled each of his servant's accounts. He was pleased at the servants that doubled their money. He recognized their good stewardship over a few things and promised to make them rulers over many things (v.20-23).

When the third servant presented the same talent originally given to him, his master became outraged and ordered him to give his money to the servant who was given five talent (v24-28).

This parable describes the consequences of two attitudes of Jesus Christ's return. The person who diligently prepares for this joyous occasion by investing his/her time and talents to serve God will be rewarded. The lazy and wasteful person who has no heart to serve God will suffer lack. **Stewardship is a privilege, not a right!**

Biblical References

Colossians 1:16
John 1:14a
Proverbs 18:9
Matthew 25:21

John 1:1
1 Corinthians 10:26
Proverbs 3:9

Assignment
How to Love God through Stewardship?

1. If God is the creator and owner of **"all that is,"** what does that make us? (Explain)

2. In addition to gaining the trust of the Lord, what is the other benefit of loving God through stewardship? (Explain)

3. What did the Garden of Eden represent as it relates to Adam? What does it represent to us?

4. Make a list of all of the things that God has placed under your stewardship (e.g. your body, children, home, car, job, etc.) For each item listed, determine if you have exercised Godly stewardship over those things.

Once you have identified the area(s) in your life that need improvement, confess and repent of your sin(s), then ask God for His forgiveness. Lastly, study God's Word to learn how to become a better steward over the things for which He has blessed you.

By using the steps outlined in the introduction of this book, interpret the bold words in the following scripture, Psalms 89:11:

> "The **heavens** are thine, the **earth** also is thine: as of the **world** and the **fulness** thereof, thou hast **founded** them."

Chapter 6
How Do We Love Ourselves?

"For ye are bought with a price: therefore glorify God in your body, and in your spirit, which are God's."

1 Corinthians 6:20

Before we can learn how to love ourselves, we must know who we are and to whom we belong.

Who Are We?

God's Word teaches us that we are made in the image and likeness of God. Genesis 1:26a reads:

"And God said, Let us make man in our image, after our likeness..."

We also learn that God is a Spirit. John 4:24 reads:

"God is a Spirit: and they that worship Him must worship Him in spirit and in truth."

Since God is a Spirit and we are made in the likeness and image of Him, we are spirits as well. In order to properly function on earth, God gave us a body (Genesis 2:7a) and soul (Genesis 2:7b).

To Whom Do We Belong?

In chapter 5, we learned that God is the owner of everything and everyone. As previously cited in Psalms 24:1:

"The earth is the Lord's, and the fulness thereof; the world, and they that dwell therein."

The operative phrase in this verse of scripture is "they that dwell therein." Whether we choose to believe in God or not, He is the Creator of all mankind, as well as all that is around us. As a matter of fact, Apostle Paul teaches us that God paid the ultimate price for our salvation, the sacrifice of His only begotten Son. 1 Corinthians 6:20 reads:

"For ye are bought with a price: therefore glorify God in your body, and in your spirit, which are God's."

Since we are neither the creator nor the owner of ourselves, we must learn how to exercise proper stewardship over God's greatest creation.

How Do We Love Ourselves?

We love ourselves by:

1. Accepting "The" free gift of eternal spiritual life, Jesus!

John teaches us that God loved us so much that He sacrificed His only begotten Son for our salvation. Those of us that choose to accept this precious gift will receive everlasting or eternal spiritual life (John 3:16).

When we as followers of Christ die, our flesh returns to the ground from whence it came (Genesis 3:19) and our spirit returns to Heaven to be with the Father, to live forever.

2.   Feeding our spirit the Word of God.

When we accept Jesus Christ as our personal Lord and Savior and become new creatures in Christ or born-again, our spirit is in its infancy stage, similar to a newborn child. In order for our spirit to grow and mature, we must consistently feed it the Word of God, so it will not return to its weakened state, before our salvation. 1 Peter 2:2 reads:

"As newborn babes, desire the sincere milk of the word, that ye may grow thereby:"

As we continue to grow and mature spiritually, we need more than milk or baby food to sustain and strengthen us. Hebrews 5:13-14a reads:

"For every one that useth milk is unskilful (inexperienced) in the word of righteousness: for he is a babe. But **strong meat** *belongeth to them that are of full age,"*

The Greek translation of *strong meat* is "stereos trophe," which means solid nourishment. When we were first born, our body could only handle breast milk or some type of baby formula. As we grew older, we were able to digest foods with a stronger consistency and eventually solid table food.

If as adults we attempted to survive off of formula or baby food alone, our body would become weak and eventually die. The same holds true with our spirit, when we do not feed it the Word of God.

3.   **Protecting our spirit from the devil.**

Apostle Paul teaches us that we must cover our spirit with the complete armor of God, so that we are well equipped to do battle against Satan and his army. Ephesians 6:11-17 reads:

> *"Put on the whole armour of God, that ye may be able to stand against the wiles of the devil. For we wrestle not against flesh and blood, but against principalities, against powers, against the rulers of the darkness of this world, against spiritual wickedness in high places. Wherefore take unto you the whole armour of God, that ye may be able to withstand in the evil day, and having done all, to stand. Stand therefore, having your loins girt about with truth, and having on the breastplate of righteousness; And your feet shod with the preparation of the gospel of peace; Above all, taking the shield of faith, wherewith ye shall be able to quench all the fiery darts of the wicked. And take the helmet of salvation, and the sword of the Spirit, which is the word of God..."*

Once we accepted Jesus Christ as our personal Lord and Savior, we became an enemy and target of the devil. In order to withstand these spiritual attacks, which manifest themselves in the natural, we must depend on the strength of God and cover our spirit with every piece of God's armour and never take them off!

Paul also encourages us to remain in a state of prayer, never leaving the presence of God and communicating with the Father via the power of the Holy Spirit, which is in us. Ephesians 6:18a reads:

"Praying always with all prayer and supplication in the Spirit..."

As followers of Jesus Christ, we are on the front line of the battle (earth), using our walkie-talkies (Holy Spirit) to receive instructions from the General (God), who is located back at headquarters (Heaven).

4. Walking after the Spirit, not after the flesh.

Apostle Paul instructs us to allow the Spirit of God to lead, guide and direct our life and not the desires of our flesh. Galatians 5:16 reads:

*"This I say then, **Walk** in the Spirit, and ye shall not fulfil the lust of the flesh."*

In the context of this scripture, the Greek translation of *walk* is "peripateo," which means to live. Living after the Spirit involves the desire to hear from God, having the readiness to obey His Word and the sensitivity to distinguish between the voice of God and your own fleshly carnal mind.

Paul encourages us to live each day controlled and guided by the Holy Spirit. The Holy Spirit allows God's Word to flow from our heart, to our mind, to our speech and to our actions.

How do we love ourselves? By treating our spirit just like we would care for a newborn baby. We must give our baby nourishment (The Word). We must cover and protect our baby with clothing and shelter (God's Whole Armor). Lastly, we must lead and guide our baby (Walking After the Spirit).

What are the Benefits to Loving Myself?

Once we are able to demonstrate our love for ourselves by accepting Jesus Christ as our personal Lord and Savior, feeding our spirit the Word of God, protecting our spirit from the devil and walking after the Holy Spirit, we can live that great life the Jesus promised us. John 10:10b reads:

"I (Jesus) am come that they might have life, and that they might have it more abundantly."

The "they" that Jesus is referring to is those whom that have accepted Him as their personal Lord and Savior. Contrary to popular belief, salvation is a **journey**, and not a **destination**. Too many "saved" folks focus solely on going to Heaven and miss the great opportunity to live a super abundant life according to the Word of God.

Biblical References

Genesis 1:26a, 27
1 Corinthians 10:26
2 Timothy 2:15
Romans 8:5-6

John 4:24
Romans 8:32
2 Corinthians 10:3-5

Assignment
How Do We Love Ourselves?

1. In what order did God create the following: our soul, spirit and body? (Genesis chapter 1-2)

2. Name three ways in which we can love ourselves.

How Do We Love Ourselves?

3. In Ephesians 6:18a, what did Apostle Paul mean by **"praying always with all prayer and supplications in the Spirit?"** Is he suggesting that we walk with our eyes closed, our hands folded and speaking in tongues or does it mean something different? Explain.

4. Apostle Paul encourages us to walk after the Spirit and not after the flesh. Determine which one is leading us.

Take out a blank sheet of paper. Fold it in half, the long way, thus creating two columns. At the top of the left column, write the word **Spirit** and on the top right column write the word **flesh.**

Next, take an inventory of your life. Think of the people with whom you associate or fellowship, the places you visit and the activities that occupy your life.

As you begin to think of those people, places and activities determine if they are more pleasing to your spirit and or to your flesh.

Lastly, place each of the items in the appropriate column. Which of the two lists is the longest will determine if you are living after the Spirit or the flesh.

By using the steps outlined in the introduction of this book, interpret the bold words in the following scripture, Ephesians 6:13-17:

> Wherefore take unto you the **whole armour** of God, that ye may be able to **withstand** in the evil day, and having done all, to **stand**. Stand therefore, having your **loins girt** about with truth, and having on the **breastplate** of **righteousness**; And your feet **shod** with the **preparation** of the **gospel** of peace; Above all, taking the **shield** of **faith**, wherewith ye shall be able to **quench** all the **fiery darts** of the **wicked**. And **take** the **helmet** of **salvation**, and the **sword** of the Spirit, which is the word of God"

Chapter 7

How Do We Love Our Parents?

"Children, obey your parents in the Lord: for this is right."
Ephesians 6:1

Who Are Our Parents?

Webster's defines a parent as "one that begets or brings forth its offspring." A biological parent best fits this definition.

In addition to a biological mother and father, a parent can be defined as a guardian, one who may or may not be related to the child, but has assumed responsibility of the total well being of the child. A person who adopts someone's child(ren), best describes a legal guardian or foster parent.

Lastly, a parent can be defined as any one in an authoritative role over the child's life, such as a teacher, school bus driver, government official, or even a next door neighbor. Although these people are not ultimately responsible for the total well being of our children, they do, however, play a significant role in developing our future leaders.

How Do We Love Our Parents?

God's Word teaches us that as children of any age, we must adhere to our parent's instructions. Ephesians 6:1 reads:

*"Children **obey** your parents in the Lord: for this is right."*

In the context of this scripture, the Greek translation of *obey* is "hupakouo", which means to listen attentively, to heed or conform to a command or authority.

We are to reveal our love to our parents just as we do in our relationship with God by receiving and following their instructions. John 14:21a reads:

"He that hath my commandments, and keepeth them, he it is that loveth me..."

We express our love for Jesus and our parents by obeying their commandments and teachings. As I stated in an earlier chapter, love is more than kind words. It is a commitment to those words and the action that follows. In order to love both Christ and our parents, we must prove it by following their instructions.

In addition to obeying our parents, we should love them by respecting their position in our lives. God instructs the believer directly in Exodus 20:12a:

*"**Honour** thy father and thy mother:"*

In the context of this scripture, the Hebrew translation of *honour* is "kabed", which means to glorify or show respect. Whether or not our parents have accepted Jesus Christ as their personal Lord and Savior, God has placed them in our lives to provide leadership, guidance and direction. Despite whatever feelings we may have for our parents, we as Christian children must honor and obey them.

As our parents grow older, we will have the opportunity to once again reveal our love for them by sacrificing our time, space and money as they did for us.

Although God's Word instructs us to love our parents by obeying and honoring them, we should not love our mother and father more than Jesus. Matthew 10:37a reads:

"He that loveth father or mother more than me is not worthy of me..."

The love we reveal to our parents is a gift given by God, but even this love can be selfishly motivated and used as an excuse not to serve God or follow His commandments.

What Are the Benefits of Loving Our Parents?

As a result of obeying and honoring (respecting) our parents, God promises us a long life. He tells us in Exodus 20:12:

*"**Honour** thy father and thy mother: that thy days may be long upon the land which the Lord thy God giveth thee."*

This is the first commandment with a promise attached.

In addition to long life, God promises peace to reign in our lives. Proverbs 3:1-2 reads:

"My son, forget not my law; but let thine heart keep my commandments: For length of days, and long life, and peace, shall they add to thee."

This promise of length of days, long life and peace is not meant just for us, but for our descendants as well.

The Story of Ruth

The book of Ruth tells the wonderful story of how Ruth honored and obeyed Naomi, her mother-in-law, despite their religious and cultural differences. Ruth 1:16-17 reads:

*"And **Ruth** said, Entreat [beg] me not to leave thee, or to return from following after thee: for whither thou goest, I will go; and where thou lodgest, I will lodge: thy people shall be my people, and thy God my God: Where thou diest, will I die, and there will I be buried: the Lord do so to me, and more also, if ought but death part thee and me."*

In the context of this scripture, the Hebrew translation of *Ruth* is "ruwth," which means "friend". Ruth definitely lived up to the meaning of her name.

As a result of Ruth's love and faithfulness toward her mother-in-law and God, Ruth was blessed with a peaceable long life that stretched to the house of David and to the time of Jesus and to those persons who have accepted Jesus Christ as their personal Lord and Savior.

I encourage you to read and study the book of Ruth, which illustrates the love shown to a parent from a child.

How Do We Love Our Parents?

Biblical References

Colossians 3:20
Proverbs 1:8
Luke 4:8
Proverb 6:22

John 14:15
Matthew 15:4
Proverbs 1:7

Assignment
How Do I Love My Parents?

1. How do we reveal our love toward God as well as our parents? (John 14:21a)

2. What did Jesus mean, when He said, **"He that loveth father or mother more than me is not worthy of me:"**? (Matthew 10:31a)

3. What are the benefits of honoring and obeying our parents?

4. Match the following biblical characters with their obedient and respectful behavior or disobedient and disrespectful behavior toward their parents, guardians or leaders, by placing the letter in the space provided:

1. _____Ruth
   Ruth 1:15-17

A. Brought to life what Jesus taught us about loving parents more than Him, by saving the life of his father's enemy, David, soon to be king of Israel, anointed by God.

2. _____Hophni and Phinehas
   1 Samuel 2:12, 23-25

B. Dishonored his father David, by raping his half sister, David's daughter.

3. _____Jonathan
   1 Samuel 20:1-4

C. After the death of her husband, this person decided to stay with her mother-in law, forsaking her cultural and religious background.

4. _____Solomon
1 Kings 2:1-3

D. Despite their father Noah's drunkenness, they honored Noah by walking into his tent backwards to cover his nakedness.

5. _____Amnon
2 Samuel 13:14-15

E. Despite feeling unworthy, he obeyed Jesus, his natural and spiritual leader, by baptizing Him.

6. _____Shem and Japheth
Genesis 9:23

F. Disobeyed his father, David, by not obeying his instructions to always follow the Lord.

7._____John the Baptist
Matthew 3:13-14

G. Dishonored their father, Eli, by sleeping with women in the church.

By using the steps outlined in the introduction of this book, interpret the bold words in the following scripture, Exodus 20:12:

"**Honour** thy **father** and thy **mother**: that thy **days** may be **long** upon the **land** which the **Lord** thy God **giveth** thee."

Chapter 8

How Do We Love Our Spouse?

"But I would have you know, that the head of every man is Christ; and the head of the woman is the man; and the head of Christ is God."

Corinthians 11:3

A "State" of Contentment

As a single person contemplating marriage, it is important to maximize our role as an unmarried man of valor or as a virtuous woman of God.

Apostle Paul teaches us to be satisfied at any level of our life. Philippians 4:11-12 reads:

> *"Not that I speak in respect of want: for I have learned, in whatsoever state I am, therewith to be content. I know both how to be abased, and I know how to abound: every where and in all things I am instructed both to be full and to be hungry, both to abound and to suffer need."*

The union (marriage) between a man and woman is a wonderful institution created and ordained by God. However, if entered into hastily, as a result of loneliness, peer pressure or any other ungodly reason, that wedding day we were so looking forward to will become a day we wish had never occurred.

Prior to saying, "I do," we need to take a personal inventory of our life. If we are not living up to the standards according to the Word of God as a single person, clearly we are not ready to accept the responsibilities and challenges as a husband or wife.

Unfortunately, too many of us weigh down our new mates with unnecessary baggage, such as a bad attitude, outrageous debt, children born out of wedlock, sexually transmitted diseases, etc.

As a single person, we have the wonderful opportunity to present our future mate with the **ideal** gift. Before courtship we should be born-again Christians, filled with the Holy Spirit, content with whom and where we are in life, following after Jesus Christ, possessing an intimate relationship with God.

I encourage you to re-read chapter 6, entitled, "How Do We Love Ourselves?" In that chapter, we learned who we are according to God's Word and to Whom we belong. We also realized that in order for each of us to love ourselves, we must accept the free gift of salvation; feed our spirit the Word of God; protect our spirit from the devil and walk after the Spirit and not after the flesh.

How Do We Choose a Husband or Wife?

Prior to accepting Jesus Christ as our personal Lord and Savior, many of us selected our mate based on their external features, such as a shapely body, complexion of skin, texture of hair and so on, ignoring the internal characteristics or spirit, which can not be seen with the natural eye.

If we chose our mate solely based on the physical attributes that originally attracted us, we missed the opportunity to see if we are compatible spiritually.

The prophet Jeremiah teaches us that prior to being born, God not only knew and set us apart for his specific use, He gave us a purpose and an assignment, which was to be fulfilled here on earth. Jeremiah 1:5 reads:

> *"Before I formed thee in the belly I knew thee; and before thou camest forth out of the womb I sanctified thee, and I ordained thee a prophet unto the nations."*

God may not have called us and our mate to become a couple. If we are not careful, we may actually hinder God's plan for us and our prospective mate.

We must take our eyes off of the other person and first seek God and His kingdom for guidance. God knows the things we need to satisfy us both spiritually and naturally. Matthew 6:32–33 reads:

> *"(For after all these things [food, drink, clothing] do the Gentiles seek): for your heavenly Father knoweth that ye have need of all these things. But seek ye first the kingdom of God, and his righteousness; and all these things shall be added unto you."*

Solomon teaches us that God will lead, guide and direct us if we put all of our trust in Him and recognize God in every aspect of our lives. In Proverbs 3:5–6, he writes:

"Trust in the Lord with all thine heart; and lean not unto thine own understanding. In all thy ways acknowledge Him, and He shall direct thy paths."

What Are the Roles of a Husband and Wife?

The role of the husband (man) is to provide for, maintain and protect his family, home and environment. This role is God-given as described in Genesis 2:5,8, 15:

*"And every plant of the field before it was in the earth, and every herb of the field before it grew: for the Lord God had not caused it to rain upon the earth, and there was not a man to till the ground. And the Lord God planted a garden eastward in Eden; and there he put the man whom He had formed. And the Lord God took the man, and put him into the Garden of Eden to **dress** it and to **keep** it."*

In the context of this scripture, the Hebrew translation of *dress* and *keep* is "abad" and "shamar," which means to work and guard or protect.

The garden created by God was an environment enabling Adam and his family to live, grow and prosper. For us the garden represents our home, place of employment and all of the other items with which God has blessed us.

Just like Adam, God expects the **male** seed to not only exercise proper stewardship over his environment, but he must protect his family in this environment as well.

The role of the wife (woman) is to assist or help her husband accomplish the assignment given to her husband (man) by God. Genesis 2:18 reads:

"And the Lord God said, It is not good that the man should be alone; I will make him an help meet for him"

In the context of this scripture, the Hebrew translation of *meet* is "ezer," which means aid.

God did not create Eve (woman) just because Adam (man) was lonely and needed some companionship. Eve (woman) was created by God to assist her husband (Adam) in accomplishing the task given to him by God, which is to dress and keep the garden.

It is a dangerous thing for a man and a woman to enter into a marriage without understanding and/or knowing their respective roles as husband and wife. It is equally dangerous for a man to marry a woman who does not realize she is called to assist him or for a woman to hook up with a man who is not prepared to lead.

Today, if every man accepted his role of head of the household and every woman helped her husband meet the needs of the household, divorce would not be as prevalent.

How Do We Love Our Husband or Wife?

In order to reveal their true love for one another, both husband and wife must be subject one to another, as unto God. Ephesians 5:21 reads:

"Submitting yourselves one to another in the fear of God."

The Greek translation of *submitting* is "huptasso," which means to subordinate or obey.

The devil has done a masterful job of perverting the true meaning of submit. It does not mean we become an indentured servant to our spouse.

It is essential to understand that submission is not surrender, withdrawal, or apathy. It does not mean inferiority, because God created male and female in HIS image (Genesis 1:27) and both have equal value. Submission is a mutual commitment with God and our spouse.

Apostle Paul goes on to teach us in Ephesians 5:23 and 1 Corinthians 11:3 that Jesus is to submit to God, as man submits to Jesus and woman is to submit to man. 1 Corinthians 11:3 reads:

"But I would have you know, that the head of every man is Christ; and the head of the woman is the man; and the head of Christ is God."

Jesus Christ, although equal to God the Father, submitted Himself to carry out the plan for salvation. Likewise, although equal to one another under God, both the husband and wife must submit to one another.

Submission is rarely a problem in homes where both the husband and wife have an intimate relationship with Christ and are willing to obey His commandments and teachings.

A wife is to reveal her love toward her husband by willingly following her husband's leadership in Christ. This instruction appears in Ephesians 5:22:

"Wives, submit yourselves unto your own husbands, as unto the Lord."

The operative phrase in that verse of scripture is **"as unto the Lord."** It's not the wife's role to be a slave to her husband, but to serve him as she would serve the Lord.

A husband is to demonstrate his love for his wife by denying his own selfish desires, sacrificing and completely giving of himself as Christ gave of Himself to the church. Ephesians 5:25 reads:

> *"Husbands, love your wives, even as Christ also loved the church, and gave himself for it..."*

Christ loved the church so much, He literally gave His life for it. He accepted His role as the "perfect sacrifice" and followed God's commandments, even unto death. A born-again husband **must** be willing to sacrifice everything for his wife.

Apostle Paul also instructs husbands to love their wives as they love themselves. Ephesians 5:28-29 reads:

> *"So ought men to love their wives as their own bodies. He that loveth his wife loveth himself. For no man ever yet hated his own flesh; but nourisheth and cherisheth it, even as the Lord the church..."*

A husband is to care for his wife as he takes care of his own body. Christian Sisters, before saying, "I do", examine how well your prospective mate exercises Godly stewardship over his body. If he abuses his body by poisoning it with drugs, alcohol and/or an illicit sex life, that is a clear sign that he will not treat YOU any better.

If your spouse is able to apply these life-changing principles to his or her life there is a greater propensity he or she will obey God's Word as it relates to loving you.

Apostle Paul also teaches us that a husband and wife are of one flesh, sharing their affection with one another, not withholding sexual intimacy from the other, except during a mutually agreed upon period of time. 1 Corinthians 7:3-5 instructs:

> *"Let the husband render unto the wife due benevolence: and likewise also the wife unto the husband. The wife*

> *hath not power of her body, but the husband: and likewise also the husband hath not power of his own body, but the wife. Defraud ye not one the other, except it be with consent for a time, that ye may give yourselves to fasting and prayer; and come together again, that Satan tempt you not for your incontinency (lack of self control).*

It's the responsibility of the husband and wife to care for the needs of their spouse, which includes, but is not limited to sexual desires. One of the reasons God created marriage was to provide a method by which a **married** couple can satisfy these natural sexual desires and strengthen the husband and wife against sexual temptation.

Jesus paid the ultimate price for our body. As a result, we spiritually belong to God. However, when we enter into the union of marriage, physically our body belongs to our spouse. **Two people become one.**

How Do We Love Our Unsaved Husband or Wife?

Apostle Paul teaches us that if we are married to an unbeliever who chooses to stay with us, we are to be a Godly example for them to follow. Although the unbelieving spouse does not realize it, they are receiving the blessing of God via their saved husband or wife.

On the other hand, if the unsaved spouse wishes to leave and his or her born-again mate has done all they could do to convince them to stay (short of giving up their salvation), Paul instructs them to allow their spouse to leave. 1 Corinthians 7:12-15 reads:

"But to the rest speak I, not the Lord: If any brother hath a wife that believeth not, and she be pleased to dwell with him, let him not put her away. And the woman which hath an husband that believeth not, and if he be pleased to dwell with her, let her not leave him. For the unbelieving husband is sanctified by the wife, and the unbelieving wife is sanctified by the husband: else were your children unclean; but now are they holy. But if the unbelieving depart, let him depart. A brother or a sister is not under bondage in such cases: but God hath called us to peace.

CAUTION! *Do not interpret verse 15 as God's instructing us to abandon our mate simply* **because** *they are unsaved.* As members of the Body of Christ, our job is to continue the earthly ministry of Jesus Christ, which is to seek and save those who are lost, even if it's our husband or wife. **In order for a husband and wife to have a successful marriage, both must be submitted to Jesus Christ, as well as one to another.**

What Are the Benefits of Loving Our Spouse?

By loving our spouse according to the Word of God, we will be able to:

1. **Maintain a pure and innocent relationship with our spouse.** Genesis 2:25 reads:

   "*And they (Adam and Eve) were both naked, the man and his wife, and were not ashamed.*"

Prior to the fall of Adam, he and his wife, Eve were able to look at each other with their "spiritual eyes," without shame, guilt or embarrassment. They were able to ignore the fact that both of them were naked and focused on their God-given role and responsibilities as husband and wife.

Once Adam disobeyed God and ate of the tree of knowledge of good and evil (Genesis 3:6), he and Eve immediately realized they were both naked and their fellowship with each other was no longer pure and innocent. Genesis 3:7 reads:

"And the eyes of them both were opened, and they knew that they were naked; and they sewed fig leaves together, and made themselves aprons.

As a result of Adam's disobedience, he and Eve could no longer experience the perfect fellowship they once shared with one another. By taking a bite of that "forbidden" fruit, Adam placed Eve above God and chose to obey her and not the commandments of God.

In order to maintain a pure and innocent fellowship with our mates, we must **first** obey the statutes, judgements, commandments and instructions of God, as it relates to every aspect of our life. Then we must allow the Spirit of God to lead, guide and teach us how to love our spouse within the framework of His Word.

2. **Maintain an open line of communication between God and us.** 1 Peter 3:7 reads:

"Likewise, ye husbands, dwell with them according to knowledge, giving honor unto the wife, as unto the weaker vessel and as being heirs together of the grace of life; that your prayers be not hindered."

Although Peter is specifically addressing husbands, these instructions apply to the wife as well. By loving our mate according to the Word of God, our communication with God will not be cut off. If a man or woman **chooses** not to treat his or her spouse kindly, their prayers become ineffective and their fellowship is damaged, as was the case with Adam and Eve. As we read in Genesis 3:8, which says:

"And they heard the voice of the Lord God walking in the garden in the cool of the day: and Adam and his wife hid themselves from the presence of the Lord God amongst the trees of the garden."

Both Adam and Eve knew the "deadly" consequences of eating from that tree. As a result of their sin, they lost the wonderful and complete (*spiritual and natural*) fellowship they shared with God and the open line of communication between God and mankind would be damaged forever.

3. **Experience natural, as well as a spiritual intimacy with our spouse.** Song of Solomon 6:3a reads:

"I am my beloved's, and my beloved is mine..."

Within a Christian marriage, both the husband and wife should focus on satisfying their mate's natural, emotional and spiritual needs. The entire book of Song of Solomon is an expression of love between a husband and wife, although it ultimately describes the relationship of Christ to His church.

When any kind of sin enters into a marriage, the intimacy shared between a husband and wife is immediately lost. When questioned by God, Adam blamed Eve for his act of disobedience. Genesis 3:11-12 reads:

"And He [God] said, Who told thee that thou wast naked? Hast thou eaten of the tree, whereof I commanded thee that thou shouldest not eat? And the man said, The woman whom thou gavest to be with me, she gave me of the tree, and I did eat."

No longer did Adam see Eve as a blessing from God; he accused her of being the reason for his downfall. The intimacy between a husband and wife was meant to be an unbreakable bond created by God, but in the hands of the devil, intimacy becomes a fragile and lifeless experience.

Biblical Refernces

Proverbs 15:27a
Psalms 34:9
Colossians 3:18
Ephesians 5:28

Isaiah 49:5a
Philippians 2:6-8
Colossians 3:19

Assignment
How Do We Love Our Spouse?

1. When Adam and Eve sinned in the garden, what were the consequences they experienced? (Genesis 3:7)

2. What is the role of the husband and wife? (Genesis 2:5,8,15)

3. How are husbands and wives to demonstrate their love to one another? What example are we to follow? (Ephesians 5:22, 25,28-29)

4. As we learned in this chapter, we are to present our prospective mate with "the gift" and not weigh them down with heavy personal baggage.

Whether you are single or married, make a list of those things in your life God would consider to be "baggage." Search God's Word to determine what instructions He gives concerning each of those items. Once you have overcome a "baggage" item, cross it out.

When you have completed this assignment, destroy the paper and make a covenant with God that those issues will never plague you or your (future) spouse's life again.

By using the steps outlined in the introduction of this book, interpret the bold words in the following scripture, Ephesians 5:22, 25:

> "**Wives, submit** yourselves unto your own husbands, as unto the **Lord. Husbands, love** your wives, **even** as **Christ** also loved the **church**, and **gave** himself for it"

Chapter 9

How Do We Love Our Children?

"Train up a child in the way he should go: and when he is old, he will not depart from it."

Proverbs 22:6

Before we can learn how to love our children, we must examine the meaning of the word, "child." Apostle Paul teaches us that we are to follow God as beloved children. Ephesians 5:1 reads:

*"Be ye therefore followers of God, as dear **children**..."*

In the context of this scripture, the Greek translation of *children* is "teknon," which means child as in son or daughter. Webster defines a child as an unborn or recently born person or a young person especially between infancy and youth.

In addition to its biological description, a child can be under the custodial care of a guardian, who may or may not be related to the child, but has assumed responsibility of the total well being of the child. A person who adopts someone else's child(ren), best describes this custodial relationship.

Lastly, a child can be defined as anyone under the authority of another, usually determined by a difference in age or position.

As adults, we must accept the responsibility of being Godly role models and examples for our children to follow, whether it's our own son or daughter, the child(ren) next door or any child with whom we have contact.

In addition to being a Godly role model, we must teach our children that they are spirits, made in the image and likeness of God (Genesis 1:26a, John 4:24), who lives in a body and has a living, breathing soul (Genesis 2:7).

We must also teach them that prior to being born, they had a close and personal relationship with God. He has already set them apart for His good use and gave them a purpose to carry out here on earth (Jeremiah 1:5).

Lastly, we must teach our children that God paid the ultimate price for their salvation, by sacrificing His only begotten Son (1 Corinthians 6:20). We must teach them that all who believe in Jesus shall not die, but have eternal life (John 3:16).

How Do We Love Our Children?

1. **We must teach our children to follow God and His teachings.** God instructed Moses to gather the "children" of Israel so that they could hear from, learn of and fear God. Once they developed a close and personal relationship with God, they were to teach all that they had learned to their children. Deuteronomy 31:12-13 reads:

"Gather the people together, men, and women, and children, and thy stranger that is within thy gates, that they may hear, and that they may learn, and fear the Lord your God, and observe to do all the words of this law: And that their children, which have not known any thing, may hear, and learn to fear the Lord your God, as long as ye live in the land whither ye go over Jordan to possess it."

When our children are born into this world, they are totally dependent upon us both naturally and spiritually. It is our responsibility to provide them with spiritual and natural knowledge, based on what we have learned from God's Word.

2. **We must be a Godly example for our children to follow.** Not only are we to teach our children to obey God and His Word, we must give them an example to follow. Deuteronomy 6:4–7 reads:

*"Hear, O Israel: The Lord our God is one Lord: And thou shalt love the Lord thy God with all thine heart, and with all thine soul, and with all thy might. And these words, which I command thee this day, shall be in thine heart: And thou shalt **teach** them **diligently** unto thy children, and shalt talk of them when thou sittest in thine house, and when thou walkest by the way, and when thou liest down, and when thou risest up."*

The operative phrase in this verse of scripture is **"teach them diligently."** In this context of scripture, *teach* and *diligently* have the same Hebrew translation, which is "shanac," meaning inculcate or to teach by frequent repetitions.

As parents, we must remove the cliché "Don't Do As I Do, Do As I Say" from our paradigm. We must stop sending conflicting messages to our children. We must be willing to adhere to and follow the rules we set for our children. No superstar athlete, musical artist or movie star can mold or shape the behavior of our children more than WE can.

3. **We must correct our children's misbehavior through discipline.** As parents, guardians and role models, it is our responsibility to admonish our children so that they remain on the path of righteousness. Proverbs 13:24 reads:

"He that spareth [hold back] his rod [stick] hateth his son: but he that loveth him chasteneth [disciplines] him betimes [promptly]"

It's not easy for a loving parent to discipline a child, but it is necessary. A lack of discipline shows a lack of concern for the natural and spiritual development of the child. Without some type of correction, children grow up with no clear understanding of right and wrong and no Godly direction in their lives.

Apostle Paul teaches us that discipline is an act of love, not hate. Ephesians 6:4 reads:

*"And, ye fathers, **provoke** not your children to **wrath**: but bring them up in the nurture and admonition of the Lord."*

In this context of scripture, *provoke* and *wrath* have the same Greek translation, which is "paromoiazo," meaning to enrage. As stated earlier, the purpose of parental discipline is to cause our children to develop and grow in the Lord, not to hurt and discourage them. We must love our children as God loves us, by correcting them in a prompt, but loving fashion.

4. **We must leave a deposit in the earth for the next generation.** As we receive the blessings of God, we must not consume them upon the lust of our flesh, but "replenish the earth" (Genesis 1:28), so that generations to come may benefit from our labor and hard work. Proverbs 13:22a reads:

"A good man leaveth an inheritance to his children's children..."

This inheritance is not merely worldly possessions such as homes, cars, clothes and money, but we must leave our children with the inheritance of a committed lifestyle, built on the wisdom and knowledge of the Lord.

5. **We must sacrifice for our children.** We are to follow the example of God as He sacrificed His only Son, Jesus. John 3:16 reads:

"For God so loved the world, that He gave His only begotten Son, that whosoever believeth in Him should not perish, but have everlasting life."

In the similitude of God giving up His Son for our sins, we must deny our fleshly and selfish desires so that our descendants may receive all of the blessings of God.

What Are the Benefits of Loving Our Children?

The Word of God teaches us that if we instruct our children according to the laws and commandments of God, when they are old, our children will not depart from our teachings. Proverbs 22:6 reads:

*"**Train** up a child in the way he should go: and when he is old, he will not depart from it."*

The Hebrew translation of *train* is "chanak," which means discipline. If we, as parents, guardians and role models have taught our children to obey God and His commandments, we can have comfort in the fact that they will make Godly choices when faced with challenging situations.

Biblical References

Psalms 127:3
Psalms 78:4
Colossians 3:21
Proverbs 17:6

Jeremiah 1:5
Proverbs 19:18
Psalms 37:25

Assignment
How Do We Love Our Children?

1. Apostle Paul encourages us to follow God like "**dear, _____?**" Explain. (Ephesians 5:1)

2. As parents, we are to teach our children that they are a _____ that lives in a _____ and has a living breathing _____? Fill in the blanks. (Genesis 1:26, John 4:24, and Genesis 2:7)

3. As parents, what are the five (5) basic ways we reveal our love to our children?

4. Make a list of all of the children God has placed within your environment (e.g. son, daughter, niece, nephew, a

close friend's child, the child next door or a child you see on a frequent basis, etc.)

Write down the people, places and activities in your life next to the name of those children.

If any of these items you listed are causing one of those children to stumble or hinder them from God's purpose for their life, **get rid of it**, even if it is not "unrighteous or ungodly". For example, if you work more than one job, not out of necessity, but just to have a luxurious lifestyle. Unfortunately, you're always scheduled to work during your child's extra curricular activities. Although you've earned the right to have those luxuries, you're missing out on precious time with your family. **Solution?** Adjust your lifestyle, so that you do not have to work a second job, thus allowing you to spend more time with your family.

By using the steps outlined in the introduction of this book, interpret the underlined words in the following scripture, Proverbs 13:24:

"He that **spareth** his **rod hateth** his son: but he that **loveth** him **chasteneth** him **betimes**."

Chapter 10

How Do We Love Our Employer?

"I exhort therefore, that, first of all, supplications, prayers, intercessions, and giving of thanks, be made for all men; For kings, and for all that are in authority; that we may lead a quiet and peaceable life in all godliness and honesty."

1 Timothy 2:1-2

Who is Our Employer?

Webster defines an employer or boss as one who exercises control or authority over an individual or group of people. It also describes an employer as one who directs or supervises workers.

The definition of an employer not only addresses our direct supervisor, but it also includes those persons whose jobs require them to have "official" authority over us (e.g. police officers, local representatives, Senators and even the President of the United States of America).

How Do We Love Our Employer?

We should pray for our employer. Apostle Paul encourages us to pray for our employer, so that we may have an undisturbed tranquil life, governed by holiness and integrity. 1 Timothy 2:1-2 instructs:

> *"I exhort therefore, that, first of all, supplications, prayers, intercessions, and giving of thanks, be made for all men; For kings, and for all that are in authority; that we may lead a quite and peaceable life in all godliness and honesty."*

It does not make a difference if our employers has or has not accepted Jesus Christ as their personal Lord and Savior. Paul instructs us to intercede on their behalf, giving thanks to God for the contribution our employers makes in our lives.

We must be obedient unto our employer, as unto the Lord. As employees, we must obey the rules and regulations set by our employer, as we follow the laws and commandments of God. Ephesians 6:5-7 reads:

> *"Servants, be obedient to them that are your masters according to the flesh, with fear and trembling, in singleness of your heart, as unto Christ; Not with eyeservice, as menpleasers; but as the servants of Christ, doing the will of God from the heart; With good will doing service, as to the Lord, and not to men:"*

Apostle Paul encourages us to conduct ourselves with accountability and integrity while on the job. As a Christian employee, we should do our job as though Jesus Christ were our direct supervisor or manager. We should not do good work on the job just to receive a promotion, recognition or monetary rewards. We must remember that no matter for whom we work, the one we ultimately want to please is our Father in Heaven.

We must not steal from our employer. For the most part, the reason we as consumers pay more for goods and services is due to shoplifting and shrinkage. Shrinkage is defined as merchandise stolen from an employer by his/her employees.

God's Word is perfectly clear as it relates to theft in and outside of the workplace. Exodus 20:15 reads:

"Thou shalt not steal."

No matter how inviting the merchandise, if it is not your property, **DON'T TOUCH IT! LEAVE IT WHERE IT BELONGS - AT WORK!**

Joseph, the interpreter of dreams, provides a wonderful example of how not to steal from an employer. Despite being left to die by his brothers and then sold into slavery, God and man found favor with Joseph. (Genesis 39:1-3) As a result of his personal integrity and diligent work ethics, Joseph was appointed to the position of **"overseer"** or manager of Potiphar's (officer of Pharaoh) house.

Potiphar's wife had lust in her heart for Joseph and tried to seduce him on three separate occasions. Each time Joseph refused her advances and finally fled the house (Genesis 39:7-13).

Although Joseph was the overseer of Potiphar's possessions, Joseph knew that sleeping with Potiphar's wife would dishonor the Lord as well as his employer. Joseph was more concerned with pleasing the Lord than his flesh. **How many of us are willing to do the same?**

We must exercise Godly stewardship over our employers' possessions. When he was placed in the Garden of Eden,

Adam was instructed to **"dress it and keep it"** (Genesis 2:15). Adam was responsible for the development and maintenance of his work environment. When God blesses us with employment, we are to maintain the computer equipment, furniture and office supplies as though we owned the company.

We must obey our employer by trusting God, even if we are uncertain of the outcome. God instructed Moses to send a group of men into the Land of Canaan, the Promised Land, to search out the land and provide a report of its condition. Despite returning with fruit from the land, ten of the twelve men gave Moses and the congregation an **"evil report"** (Numbers 13:1-32). As a result of their bad information and unwillingness to obey Moses and trust in the Lord, God condemned the children of Israel to wander in the desert for forty (40) years.

When we are given an assignment from our employer that we do not fully understand, seek the Lord for guidance and follow His instructions.

When Is It Proper Not to Follow the Instructions of Our Employer?

It is proper not to adhere to the instructions of our employers when their instructions conflict with the Word of God. The story of the three Hebrew boys provides a vivid example of how we are to trust in the Lord, despite overwhelming circumstances.

King Nebuchadnezzar commanded everyone to worship the new golden calf he constructed (Daniel 3:5-6). Whoever did not bow down to this golden image would be thrown into the fiery furnace.

Because of their obedience and loyalty to God, the three Hebrew boys, Shadrach, Meshach and Abed-nego chose not to worship King Nebuchadnezzar's golden calf and were cast into the furnace (Daniel 3:7-23).

Needless to say, God not only delivered them from the furnace, unblemished, but He went through the fire with them. (Daniel 3:24-25).

Although our employer has "natural" authority over us, it was God who blessed us with that job and it is God whom we must serve while working for someone else.

What are the Benefits of Loving our Employer, as unto the Lord?

As a result of being a true and faithful witness in the workplace and refusing to "bow" to ungodly tasks or assignments given to us by our employer, God will give us the opportunity to change our work environment, as well as the heart of our employer, for the better.

King Nebuchadnezzar was so amazed and astonished by what he had witnessed that he recognized God as the most high God and instructed all the inhabitants of Babylon not to speak against God. In addition, due to their obedience, the three Hebrew boys were given a promotion in the Babylonian government (Daniel 3:26-30).

If we are obedient to God's commandments and instructions, He will not only bless us with employment, He will also promote us!

Biblical References

Romans 13:1 Colossians 3:22-23
Ephesians 4:28 Matthew 25:21
Numbers 14:37 Proverbs 3:5-6
Psalms 37:23

Assignment
How Do I Love My Employer?

1. What are three of the ways we are to reveal our love towards our employer?

2. When is it proper not to follow the instructions of our employer?

3. How did the three Hebrew boys honor God by not obeying King Nebuchadnezzar?

4. Make a list of the ways you can better represent the Body of Christ in the workplace. You might start to arrive at work on time or reimburse your company for the office supplies you "stole" out of the supply closet. Whatever comes to your mind, make a commitment to honor God on your job.

5. **Extra Credit:** Has your employer ever asked you do to something that conflicts with the Word of God? How did you handle it? Knowing what you know now, what would you do differently?

By using the steps outlined in the introduction of this book, interpret the bold words in the following scripture, Ephesians 6:5-7:

> "**Servants**, be **obedient** to them that are your **masters according** to the **flesh**, with **fear** and **trembling**, in **singleness** of your **heart**, as unto **Christ**; Not with **eyeservice**, as **menpleasers**; but as the servants of Christ, doing the will of God from the heart; With **good** will doing **service**, as to the Lord, and not to men..."

Chapter 11

How Do We Love our Friends?

"A friend loveth at all times,..."
Proverbs 17:17a

Who Are Our Friends?

Just like "love," the word "friend" has been misused and abused. Once again it seems as though the devil has done a masterful job at perverting the true meaning of friendship.

Webster defines a friend as one attached to another by affection or esteem. In the gospel of John and Matthew, we learned that Jesus called Lazarus, the man He raised from the dead and Judas Iscariot, the disciple who betrayed Him, His **friends**. How could both of these men be considered a friend of Jesus Christ? Let's take a look...

While Jesus was ministering to a group of religious leaders in the Temple, a friend of Jesus', named Lazarus had fallen ill and died. John 11:3 and 11 read:

*"Therefore his [Lazarus'] sisters sent unto Him [Jesus], saying, Lord, behold, he whom thou lovest is sick. These things said He: and after that He saith unto them, Our **friend** Lazarus sleepth (dead); but I go, that I may awake (raise) him out of sleep."*

The Greek word for *friend* used in this context of scripture is "philos," which means dear, fond or friendly. Webster defines dear as loved and cherished, greatly valued and precious.

Obviously, Jesus considered Lazarus to be a very close and personal friend. But, what of Judas Iscariot? Surely Jesus could not speak of the man who betrayed Him in the same regard as Lazarus.

After praying in the garden of Gethsemane, Jesus calls out to Judas as they came to arrest Him. Matthew 26:50 reads:

*"And Jesus said unto him [Judas], **Friend**, wherefore art thou come? Then came they, and laid hands [seized] on Jesus, and took him."*

The Greek word for *friend* used in this context of scripture is "hetairos," which means a comrade. Webster defines comrade as a companion, friend or associate. We associate with people due to a common interest, task or environment, such as the workplace.

Similar to our co-workers assisting us in completing an assignment at work, Jesus recognized Judas' role as a crucial element to finishing His assignment from God. Jesus prayed before Judas betrayed Him in John 17:12:

"While I was with them in the world, I kept them in thy name: those that thou gavest me I have kept, and

none of them is lost, but the son of perdition [Judas]; that the Scripture might be fulfilled."

Jesus knew that if Judas had not betrayed Him, His Father's gift of salvation to all of us would be hindered.

Whether it's the person you consider to be your best friend or that back-stabbing co-worker you can't tolerate, our Heavenly Father will use them both to continue Jesus' earthly mission, which is to "seek and save that which is lost."

How Do We Love our Friends?

WE MUST SACRIFICE FOR OUR FRIENDS. Jesus teaches us that there is no greater love that we can show than by putting the lives of others before our own selfish wants and desires. John 15:13 teaches us:

"Greater love hath no man than this, that a man lay down his life for his friends."

We can lay down our life for a friend by helping when it is not convenient, by giving when it hurts or devoting energy to other's problems or circumstances other than our own. (Philippians 2:3-4)

We must be an inspiration for our friends. Solomon instructs us to encourage one another to increase in our knowledge and application of the Word of God. Proverbs 27:17 reads:

"Iron sharpeneth iron; so a man sharpeneth the countenance of his friend."

In order for a knife to be sharpened, it must come in contact with another metal object, thus causing friction. To prevent the knife from becoming dull, we must sharpen it on a frequent basis.

The same holds true with human beings. We must challenge each other and stimulate thought. It is crucial that we do not involve our egos in conversations and know how to challenge ideas and not the person.

We must support our friends in their time of need. Apostle Paul teaches us to help our brothers and sisters in the Body of Christ when they have fallen in sin, which could cause us to fall as well. Paul also instructs us to lighten their load, by helping them to carry it. Galatians 6:1-2 reads:

"Brethren, if a man be overtaken in a fault, ye which are spiritual, restore such an one in the spirit of meekness; considering thyself, lest thou also be tempted. Bear ye one another's burdens, and so fulfil the law of Christ."

As members of the Body of Christ, it is our responsibility to humbly and gently reach out to a person who has fallen and is in need of our assistance.

We must be loyal to our friends. Despite the circumstance or situation, the Word of God encourages us to always "be there" for our friends. Proverbs 17:17a reads:

"A friend loveth at all times..."

A genuine friendship is evidenced by steadfast loyalty. Too many of us are fair-weather friends. We stick around when the relationship benefits us and leave when there is nothing for us to gain. Despite all of our shortcomings, God promised to **"never leave us, nor forsake us"** (Hebrews 13:5). We must make the same pledge to our friends.

We must never gossip about our friends. As our friends struggle to deal with certain situations in their life, we sometimes have a tendency to talk about them behind their backs. The Word of God warns us of the damaging effects gossip will have on a relationship between best friends. Proverbs 16:28b reads:

"...and a whisperer separateth chief (close) friends"

If our friend or anyone who trusts us decides to share personal information with us, that does not give us the right to share their personal information with anyone else.

We will surely damage our friendships by gossiping about our friends. What if our Father in Heaven told others what we said to Him during our confession? Most of us would not be able to show our faces in public, out of the embarrassment for our past or present sins.

We must love our friends and not their possessions. As stated earlier, we are to love our friends at all times not just when we can benefit from a material standpoint. We read in Proverbs 19:4 and 6:

"Wealth maketh many friends; but the poor is separated from his neighbor. Many will entreat [seek] the favor of the prince: and every man is a friend to him that giveth gifts."

Have you ever noticed when a person receives a lot of money, whether it is inherited, earned or won, people come out of the wood work to "claim" their piece of the pie? But once the money and fame are gone, those same people retreat, waiting for the next opportunity to freeload.

In order to be true, we must love our friends, whether they are rich or poor, popular or unpopular, have an important title behind their name or even a prison number.

We must forgive and forget the sins our friends have committed against God that have affected us. There will be times during friendships when the actions of the other person may negatively affect us. When faced with those situations, we must remember that we are **"made in the image and likeness of God"** (Genesis 1:26) and forgive our friends as God forgives us. Proverbs 17:9 reads:

"He that covereth [conceal] a transgression [sin] seeketh [searches for] love; but he that repeath a matter separateth very friends."

This proverb is not encouraging us to hide our sins, but to be willing to forgive and forget another's sins against God that may have affected us. The devil has tricked us into believing that we can forgive someone without forgetting what they have done, so we can bring up their past mistakes during a later conversation or argument.

Love, however, will keep our mouth shut, as difficult as it may be. As we **"grow up in the Lord"** (2 Peter 3:18) and become more Christ like, we will acquire God's ability to forget and forgive the actions of a friend.

What are the Benefits to Loving our Friends?

By focusing on the well-being and the needs of our friends, we pay less attention to our own fleshly needs and desires. As we learned earlier in this chapter, Jesus reminds us that **"there is no greater love than for us to lay down our life for a friend,"** (John 15:13).

The definition of a true friendship is best illustrated between Jonathan and David, the second king of Israel.

Jonathan was the prince of Israel and son of Saul, the first king.

Prior to becoming king, David and Jonathan developed a very close and loyal friendship. 1 Samuel 18:3 reads:

"Then Jonathan and David made a covenant, because he (Jonathan) loved him (David) as his own soul".

As he served in King Saul's army, David grew in power and popularity, which made Saul very jealous. As a result of this shift in power, Saul grew even angrier and on several occasions attempted to kill David (1 Samuel 18:6-9).

Instead of aiding in his father's many plots to kill David, Jonathan helped David escape from Saul. As the prince, Jonathan had every legal right to the throne of Israel, but he knew that God had anointed David as the next King of Israel. Not only did Jonathan sacrifice becoming the next king, he did everything in his power, including disobeying his father, Saul, to allow God's Will to be done. 1 Samuel 23:17-18a reads:

"And he (Jonathan) said unto him (David), Fear not: for the hand of Saul my father shall not find thee; and thou shalt be king over Israel, and I shall be next unto thee; and that also Saul my father knoweth. And they two made a covenant before the Lord..."

Jonathan, the prince of Israel, realized that David, and not he, would be the next king. As a result of his strong character, Jonathan and his love for God and David did not weaken. Jonathan chose to give up the throne of Israel rather than lose his fellowship with God and David. **What are we willing to sacrifice for a friend?**

Biblical References

John 15:15   Psalms 41:9
Ephesians 5:2   Romans 15:1
Proverbs 18:24   Proverbs 10:12
John 15:12

Assignment
How Do I Love My Friends?

1. Although Jesus called both Lazarus and Judas Iscariot His friends, Jesus had a very different relationship with the two of them. What was that difference?

2. List three of the ways we can reveal our love to our friends?

3. How did Jonathan reveal his love towards David?

4. The Word of God encourages us to demonstrate our love to our friends by: sacrificing for them; inspiring them; assisting them in times of need; being loyal to them; refusing to gossip about them; and by forgiving and forgetting their sins against God that affect us. Let's see if we meet the criteria of a true friend.

Take out a sheet of paper. Write the name of the person, whom you consider to be your best friend. Next, write the seven (7) ways we love our friends on the left side of the paper. Just below your friend's name, write the words "Pass" and "Fail", one beside the other.

As you read each criteria, determine if you have been a true friend or fair-weather friend. Place a check in the appropriate column. For every failing mark you give yourself, acknowledge and repent of your sin to God. Contact that friend and ask for him/her to forgive you, as well.

By using the steps outlined in the introduction of this book, interpret the bold words in the following scripture, Galatians 6:1-2:

> "**Brethren**, if a man be **overtaken** in a **fault**, ye which are **spiritual, restore** such an one in the **spirit** of **meekness; considering** thyself, lest thou also be **tempted. Bear** ye one another's **burdens**, and so **fulfil** the **law** of **Christ**."

Chapter 12

How Do We Love Our Enemies?

"But I say unto you which hear, Love your enemies, do good to them that hate you, Bless them that curse you, and pray for them which despitefully use you."

Luke 6:27

Who Are Our Enemies?

Webster's defines an "enemy as one seeking to injure, overthrow, or confound a person." The word that best describes an enemy is an adversary. Our greatest adversary is the devil.

Peter the Apostle warns us to be alert and watchful because our enemy, Satan is searching for those whom he may destroy. 1 Peter 5:8 reads:

"Be sober, be vigilant; because your adversary the devil, as a roaring lion, walketh about, seeking whom he may devour..."

In the context of this scripture, the Greek translation for *adversary* is "antidikos," which means opponent. Satan's mission in life is to steal God's promises, to kill our faith in Jesus and ourselves, as well as completely destroy us and God's purpose for our lives. John 10:10a reads:

"The thief cometh not, but for to steal, and to kill, and to destroy..."

Once we accept Jesus Christ as our personal Lord and Savior, and have decided to follow Him, we automatically become an enemy of the devil.

Believe it or not, even those individuals who **choose** not to be a disciple or student of Jesus Christ are Satan's enemy as well. The Word of God describes the devil, in the form of serpent in the Garden of Eden, as the most ***"subtle"*** or cunning, beast of the field. Just like a gang leader convincing a confused and lost child to join his or her gang, the devil tricks us into believing that if we run with him, he will grant us all of our wishes and lustful desires, until we are totally dependent upon him. Once he has sucked all of the life out of us and we are without strength, the devil will discard us and search for someone else to devour.

Even if we choose to be on the devil's side and serve him, we are there under false pretenses. If the devil told us up front that his plan was to steal from us, kill and destroy us, no one in his or her right mind would follow him. **No matter what the devil tells us, he is our enemy and we must "give him no place" in our life.**

How Did Satan Become Our Enemy?

Prior to God throwing him out of Heaven, Satan was Lucifer, an anointed cherub (*angel*), created by God. The Word of God describes Lucifer as being perfect in beauty, having every precious stone covering his body. He was perfect in all of his ways from the time he was created. Because of his position, Lucifer was upon the holy mountain of God, walking and talking with God (Ezekiel 28:12-15).

Unfortunately, Lucifer became obsessed with power and schemed in his heart to place himself above God. Isaiah 14:13-14 reads:

"For thou hast said in thine heart, I will ascend into heaven, I will exalt my throne above the stars of God: I will sit also upon the mount of the congregation, in the sides of the north: I will ascend above the heights of the clouds; I will be like the most High."

A soon as God read Lucifer's heart, God cast him out of heaven and to the earth. Ezekiel 28:17 reads:

"Thine heart was lifted up because of thy beauty, thou hast corrupted thy wisdom by reason of thy brightness: I will cast thee to the ground, I will lay thee before kings, that they may behold thee."

As a result of losing his position as an archangel and his banishment from Heaven, Satan considers God and all those who choose to follow Him, his enemy.

The devil has, is and will continue to go to great lengths to keep us from accepting Jesus Christ as our personal Lord and Savior. He has also employed other fallen angels and demons, who manifest themselves in the flesh in authoritative positions in our life plotting to destroy us. Ephesians 6:11-12 reads:

"Put on the whole armour of God, that ye may be able to stand against the wiles of the devil. For we wrestle not against flesh and blood, but against principalities, against powers, against the rulers of the darkness of the world, against spiritual wickedness in high places."

Satan is so cunning, he will use an unsuspecting family member, co-worker or even a complete stranger to cause us to stumble and fall out of fellowship with the Lord.

Now that we have learned that the devil is at the root cause of all evil, we need to learn how to love those persons who the devil uses against us.

How Do We Love our Enemies?

As members of the Body of Christ, Jesus is calling us to do the direct opposite of what the world has instructed us to do when someone has harmed us by words or deeds. Matthew 5:43-44 reads:

> *"Ye have heard that it hath been said, Thou shalt love thy neighbour, and hate thine enemy. But I say unto you, Love your enemies, bless them that curse you, do good to them that hate you, and pray for them which despitefully use you, and persecute you.."*

Jesus teaches us to:

Bless them that curse you. Although people may speak negatively or gossip about you, Jesus encourages us to speak well of them. When we **choose** not to engage them in a war of words, we demonstrate our love for the Triune Godhead and our willingness to be led, guided and directed by the Holy Spirit, rather than our fleshly desires.

Do good to them that hate you. One of the most effective ways to defuse someone's hostility towards you is to perform a random act of kindness towards them. Although they may be suspicious of the sincerity of your generosity and may still appear to be angry, once you have done something nice for them, their internal anger lessens almost immediately.

How Do We Love Our Enemies?

Pray for them that despitefully use and persecute you. We must remember that we do not fight against flesh and blood, but against evil spirits in powerful positions (Ephesians 6:12). The only way we can combat evil spirits, at any level, is by putting on the whole armor of God and by praying unto God to protect us and those who insult or pursue us (Ephesians 6:13-14). Instead of taking matters into our own hands, we must allow God to reveal unto our enemies the error of their ways and the consequences of their actions. **We must keep the lines of communications open between God and us.**

Apostle Paul also instructs us to attend to the natural needs of our enemies. He tells us in Romans 12:20:

"Therefore if thine enemy hunger, feed him; if he thirst, give him drink: for in so doing thou shalt heap coals of fire on his head."

Maybe our act of kindness will cause them to have a change of heart and to learn to love God and us as well.

Lastly, we are to reveal our love to our enemy by not cheering when they stumble and fall. Proverbs 24:17 reads:

"Rejoice not when thine enemy falleth, and let not thine heart be glad when he stumbleth."

God not only warns us about showing any type of outward emotion; He examines our heart to make sure we are not displaying any pleasure inwardly as well.

What Are the Benefits of Loving Our Enemies?

By loving our enemies, not only will we be abundantly repaid for our good deeds; we will be recognized as children of the Most High God. Luke 6:35a-b reads:

"But love ye your enemies, and do good, and lend, hoping for nothing again; and your reward shall be great, and ye shall be the children of the Highest..."

As a result of loving our enemies, we can become their benefactors and have our spiritual, as well as our natural needs met. In the book of 1 Samuel, chapter 30, the writer tells the story of David and how he retrieved all that was stolen from him by the Amalekites.

After receiving approval from God to **"recover all,"** David started on his journey to do battle. During his trip, He and his army found an Egyptian servant of the Amalekites, wounded and weaken from lack of food and drink. (v.13)

Despite the fact that this man was of his enemies' camp, David tended to his natural needs. As a result of this wonderful gesture, the Egyptian servant of the Amalekites, helped David recover all that was stolen from him. **We never know how or whom God will use to bless us.**

We must remember, prior to accepting Jesus Christ as our personal Lord and Savior, that we were considered an **enemy** of the Lord and He still loved us, so much so that He sent His only begotten Son to die for our sins.

Biblical References

James 4:7
Exodus 20:3
2 Corinthians 10:4
Proverbs 25:21

John 10:10
Proverbs 4:23
1 Peter 3:9

Assignment
How Do We Love Our Enemies?

1. Why did God cast Lucifer out of Heaven? (Isaiah 14:13-14)

2. What are three of the ways we can demonstrate our love toward our enemies?

3. What are we not to do when our enemy falls? Explain why. (Proverbs 24:17)

4. In Romans 12:20, Apostle Paul instructs us to care for the natural needs of our enemy. We now have a chance to apply that scripture to our life.

Think of a person that, for whatever reason, does not get along with you or has harmed you physically or emotionally. Now think of what they may need (e.g. food, clothes, money, etc). Make arrangements to deliver that item(s) to them. Lastly, forgive and forget what they have done or are doing to you.

By using the steps outlined in the introduction of this book, interpret the bold words in the following scripture, Ephesians 6:11-12:

*"Put on the **whole armour** of God, that ye may be able to **stand against** the **wiles** of the **devil**. For we **wrestle** not against **flesh** and **blood**, but against **principalities**, against **powers**, against the **rulers** of the **darkness** of this **world**, against **spiritual wickedness** in **high places.**"*

Encouragement and Advice

Throughout this entire book, I used the phrase, "accept Jesus Christ as our personal Lord and Savior" in one form or another. Until we accept the gift of God, as described in John 3:16, we will never experience love at the highest level.

If you have not yet accepted Jesus Christ as your personal Lord and Savior, here's your opportunity. In the book of Romans, Apostle Paul provides simple instructions on completing the born-again process. Romans 10:9 reads:

> *"If thou will confess with thy mouth the Lord Jesus and believe in thy heart that God raised Jesus from the dead, thou shalt be saved."*

In the context of this scripture, the Greek translation for *saved* is "sozo," which means delivered from or rescued. When we confess or acknowledge Jesus Christ as Lord with our mouth and believe or have faith in our heart that God raised Him from the dead, we are saved from an eternal damnation and gain access to God's promise of everlasting life with him. (John 3:16)

In addition to being rescued from a spiritual death, those of us who choose to accept Jesus Christ as our personal Lord and Savior, we will also be able to live an abundant life here on earth. (John 10:10)

For those of you who may still find it difficult to find the words to accept Jesus Christ as your personal Lord and Savior, I have included the following prayer of salvation:

Father, I thank you for this glorious opportunity to come to your throne and fellowship with You. Father, I thank You for allowing me to receive and understand Your Word. I thank You that Your Word brings life to my spirit and death to my fleshly desires. Father, Your Word says that if I confess my sins, You are faithful and just to forgive me of my sins and you will cleanse me from all unrighteousness. Father, I confess all of my sins and ask You to forgive me. Father, I know that if I regard any sin in my heart, You will not hear me. God please remove this filthy heart and replace it with a clean heart, and fill me with Your Spirit. Father, not only do I confess my sins, it's my prayer that I turn away from them and never allow those sins to enter into my life again. Father, Your Word says that all those who call upon the name of the Lord shall be saved, and that Jesus is Lord. So Father, I accept Jesus Christ as my personal Lord and Savior. Jesus, I confess that You are my Lord, and I believe in my heart that God the Father has raised you from the dead. I believe that You, Lord Jesus, are The Christ sent into this world so that through Your sufferings and death on the cross, my sins would be washed away. Your blood justifies me, Lord Jesus and I thank You. Lord, please place your precious Holy Spirit inside of me to teach me all things and to bring all things to my remembrance. Father, I praise and thank You for Your unconditional love, grace and mercy. In the name of Jesus, I humbly lift this prayer up to You. Amen.

Now that you have accepted Jesus Christ as your personal Lord and Savior, you **must**:

1. **Join and get involved in a Bible-believing, Bible-teaching church.** A church where the angel or pastor is not afraid to teach the uncompromising Word of God, forsaking any personal or professional relationship that may hinder the Word of God from going forth.

   The church with which I am affiliated, can and will provide you with a list of criteria for selecting a church, as well as share with you a list of churches throughout the United States and abroad that may be located near you. Please feel free to contact me via e-mail at stwnow@aol.com or write me at P.O. Box 2253, Upper Marlboro, MD, 20773-2253. I will be more than happy to share this information with you or place you in contact with the appropriate people.

2. **Feed your spirit the Word of God.** As we learned in chapter 6, we are spirits, created in the image and likeness of God. Just like our natural body or flesh hungers and survives off of food, our spirit is sustained by the Word of God. Without the consistent nourishment of the Word of God, our spirit will weaken and eventually die.

   If you are not familiar with the Bible and/or do not where to begin, I suggest you start with the Book of Proverbs. There are thirty-one (31) chapters within Proverbs, one for each day of the month. If today is the 6th day of the month, read the 6th chapter. If today is the 7th day of the month, read the 7th chapter, and so on...As your spirit grows stronger, it will hunger for more of the Word of God, at which point you will be more willing to allow the Holy Spirit to guide you through the Bible.

I also strongly suggest you enroll in some type of overview of the Bible course at your church. This will allow you to become more familiar with the Bible and less apprehensive to study the Word of God.

3. **Take a personal inventory of your life and remove all of those people,** places and activities that do not glorify God and hinder your fellowship with Him. 2 Corinthians 5:17 reads:

"Therefore if any man be in Christ, he is new creature: old things are passed away; behold, all things are become new."

When we accept the salvation of Jesus Christ, we become new people on the inside. We now have new life, both spiritually and naturally. We are no longer the same person. We are not merely turning over a new leaf; we are beginning a new life with Christ Jesus.

As a result of this change; no longer can we "run" or fellowship with people, visit the places or participate in those activities that would cause us to return to our old life, which by the way, is supposed to be dead. **(Caution: You *must* commit yourself to a daily self-examination, using the Word of God as your guide.)**

For those of you who read, **"You Can't Love God with a Dirty Bathroom,"** looking for tips on how to clean your bathroom, I am sorry if I have misled you. **Nevertheless, it is my earnest prayer that this book has been a blessing to you, in the hope that you will be a blessing to others. God Bless!**

Biblical References by Chapter

Chapter 1

Love

Psalms 136:1
Proverbs 3:12
Matthew 6:14-15
John 14:21
Romans 5:8
Romans 8:35-39
Romans 12:10
1 Corinthians 13:4

Galatians 6:10
Thessalonians 5:14
Hebrews 10:17
Hebrews 12:6
1 John 1:9
1 John 4:7-8
2 John 1:6

Chapter 2

How Do We Love and Why?

Genesis 1:26
Ezekiel 36:27
John 1:14
John 13:34-35
John 14:15-16,18
John 14:16
John 15:12
John 15:13
Romans 5:6-8
Romans 5:8

1 Corinthians 13:4
2 Corinthians 5:21
Philippians 2:3-4
Philippians 2:5-8
1 Peter 2:21-23
1 John 3:11
1 John 3:15
1 John 3:18
1 John 4:8

Chapter 3

How Do We Love God Through Obedience?

Genesis 22:10-12
Genesis 22:13
Genesis 22:15-19
Genesis 22:2-3
Proverbs 2:1-2,5
Proverbs 2:6-7
Proverbs 3:1-2
John 14:21

John 14:21a
Romans 12:9
2 Corinthians 5:7
James 1:2-3
James 2:20
1 John 2:4
1 John 3:18

Chapter 4

How Do We Love God Through Sacrifice?

Genesis 22:1-24
Mark 8:34b
Mark 8:35
Luke 14:27
John 3:16
John 12:25
John 14:21a
Romans 1:18-32
Romans 1:29-31

Romans 12:1
Romans 6:12a-13
Romans 8:32
2 Corinthians 5:17-18a
2 Corinthians 5:21
Hebrews 9:11-14
2 John 6
Revelation 1:5

Chapter 5

How Do We Love God Through Stewardship?

Genesis 1:3
Genesis 2:15-16
Psalms 24:1
Psalms 89:11
Proverbs 18:9
Proverbs 3:9
Matthew 25:14-30

Matthew 25:21
Luke 12:42
John 1:1
John 1:14a
1 Corinthians 10:26
Colossians 1:16

Chapter 6

How Do We Love Ourselves?

Genesis 1:26a
Genesis 2:7a
Genesis 2:7b
Genesis 3:19
Psalms 24:1
John 3:16
John 4:24
Romans 8:32
Romans 8:5-6

1 Corinthians 10:26
1 Corinthians 6:20
2 Corinthians 10:3-5
Galatians 5:16
Ephesians 6:11-17
Ephesians 6:18a
2 Timothy 2:15
Hebrews 5:13-14a
1 Peter 2:2

Chapter 7

How Do We Love Our Parents?

Genesis 9:23
Exodus 20:12a
Ruth 1:16-17
1 Samuel 2:12, 23-25
1 Samuel 20:1-4
1 Kings 2:1-3
2 Samuel 13:14-15
Proverbs 1:7
Proverbs 1:8
Proverbs 3:1-2

Proverbs 6:22
Matthew 3:13-14
Matthew 10:31, 37a
Matthew 15:4
Luke 4:8
John 14:15
John 14:21a
Ephesians 6:1
Colossians 3:20

Chapter 8

How Do We Love Our Spouse?

Genesis 1:27
Genesis 2:3:6-7, 25
Genesis 2:5,8,15, 18
Genesis 3:11-12
Proverbs 15:27a
Proverbs 3:5-6
Psalms 34:9
Solomon 6:3a
Isaiah 49:5a
Jeremiah 1:5

Matthew 6:32-33
1 Corinthians 11:3
1 Corinthians 7:3-5, 12-5
Ephesians 5:21
Ephesians 5:22-23,25, 28-29
Colossians 3:18-19
Philippians 2:6-8
Philippians 4:11-12
1 Peter 3:7

Biblical References by Chapter

Chapter 9

How Do We Love Our Children?

Genesis 1:26a
Genesis 1:28
Genesis 2:7
Deuteronomy 31:12-13
Deuteronomy 6:4-7
Psalms 127:3
Psalms 37:25
Psalms 78:4
Proverbs 13:22a
Proverbs 13:24

Proverbs 17:6
Proverbs 19:18
Proverbs 22:6
Jeremiah 1:5
John 3:16
John 4:24
1 Corinthians 6:20
Ephesians 5:1
Colossians 3:21

Chapter 10

How Do We Love Our Employer?

Genesis 2:15
Genesis 39:1-3
Genesis 39:7-13
Exodus 20:15
Numbers 13:1-32
Numbers 14:37
Psalms 37:23
Proverbs 3:5-6
Daniel 3:24-25

Daniel 3:26-30
Daniel 3:5-6
Daniel 3:7-23
Matthew 25:21
Romans 13:1
1 Timothy 2:1-2
Ephesians 4:28
Ephesians 6:5-7
Colossians 3:22-23

Chapter 11

How Do We Love Our Friends?

Genesis 1:26
1 Samuel 18:3, 6–9
1 Samuel 23:17–18
Psalms 41:9
Proverbs 10:12
Proverbs 16:28b
Proverbs 17:17a
Proverbs 17:9
Proverbs 18:24
Proverbs 19:4, 6
Proverbs 27:17

Matthew 26:50
John 11:3, 11–3
John 15:12, 15
John 15:13
John 17:12
Romans 15:1
Galatians 6:1–2
Ephesians 5:2
Philippians 2:3–4
Hebrews 13:5
2 Peter 3:18

Chapter 12

How Do We Love Our Enemies?

Exodus 20:3
Proverbs 4:23
Proverbs 24:17
Proverbs 25:21
Isaiah 14:13–14
Ezekiel 28:12–15
Ezekiel 28:17
Matthew 5:43–44
Luke 6:35a–b

Luke 6:27
John 10:10a
Romans 12:20
2 Corinthians 10:4
Ephesians 6:11–14
James 4:7
1 Peter 3:9
1 Peter 5:8

ABOUT THE AUTHOR

Michael was born and raised in the Washington DC metropolitan area. He is the only child of Reaugh and Marjorie White.

Upon graduation from Bishop McNamara High School, Michael entered Hampton Institute University in the fall of 1984. He received his BS Degree in Accounting in May 1988.

In addition to receiving an exceptional education, during his senior year at Hampton, Michael fell in love with Gina Flowers. In the summer of 1990 Michael and Gina became "man and wife". They both accepted Jesus Christ as their personal Lord and Savior in September 1994. Shortly thereafter, Mike and Gina joined From The Heart Church Ministries (formerly Full Gospel A.M.E. Zion Church). In July 1996, God instructed them to publish a monthly newsletter, entitled, "Spread The Word". Michael and Gina have two children, Brandyn Marie and Brian Michael. This is his first book.